"*I'll See You Tomorrow* is a profoundly human book. It poignantly describes both our vital need for human connection and all the ways we can mess it up. Yet Heather and Seth show us our missteps aren't the end of the journey, and the same is true for others. In a world where separation seems like the norm and where isolation seems inevitable, *I'll See You Tomorrow* reminds us that something so simple—healthy relationship—is utterly essential and deeply transformative."

JEMAR TISBY, PHD, *NEW YORK TIMES* BESTSELLING AUTHOR
OF *THE COLOR OF COMPROMISE* AND *HOW TO FIGHT RACISM*

"We were created for relationships. But too many of us don't have the relationships in our lives to build resilience for facing the realities of our world. In *I'll See You Tomorrow*, husband and wife Heather Thompson Day and Seth Day team up to provide tremendous help to people wanting to build relationships that will last."

ED STETZER, WHEATON COLLEGE

"Resilience is the call in our day, to stay when it feels easier to go, and to walk towards each other when it may feel easier to leave. *I'll See You Tomorrow* is a guide from some of my favorite relationship experts on the power of staying together in every kind of relationship. What could grow for you when resilience is given space to flourish?"

ANNIE F. DOWNS, *NEW YORK TIMES* BESTSELLING
AUTHOR OF *THAT SOUNDS FUN*

"*I'll See You Tomorrow* is a book for anyone who has ever wanted to walk away from a relationship. It equips you with the tools to navigate the relational challenges we face in our families, friendships, and community spaces. This book is full of practical advice and gripping storytelling, for navigating the thing we all need to thrive—human connection."

SCARLETT LONGSTREET, BLOGGER WITH *I'M THAT WIFE*

I'll See You To-mor-row

HEATHER THOMPSON DAY

SETH DAY

Building Relational Resilience When You Want to Quit

W PUBLISHING GROUP

AN IMPRINT OF THOMAS NELSON

I'll See You Tomorrow

© 2022 Heather Thompson Day and Seth Day

Published in Nashville, Tennessee, by W Publishing, an imprint of Thomas Nelson.

Thomas Nelson titles may be purchased in bulk for educational, business, fundraising, or sales promotional use. For information, please email SpecialMarkets@ThomasNelson.com.

Unless otherwise noted, Scripture quotations taken from The Holy Bible, New International Version®, NIV®. Copyright © 1973, 1978, 1984, 2011 by Biblica, Inc.® Used by permission of Zondervan. All rights reserved worldwide. www.Zondervan. com. The "NIV" and "New International Version" are trademarks registered in the United States Patent and Trademark Office by Biblica, Inc.®

Scripture quotations marked ESV are taken from the ESV® Bible (The Holy Bible, English Standard Version®). Copyright © 2001 by Crossway, a publishing ministry of Good News Publishers. Used by permission. All rights reserved.

Scripture quotations marked KJV are taken from the King James Version. Public domain.

Scripture quotations marked WEB are taken from the World English Bible™. Public domain.

ISBN 978-0-7852-9084-1 (audiobook)
ISBN 978-0-7852-9082-7 (eBook)
ISBN 978-0-7852-9081-0 (TP)

Library of Congress Cataloging-in-Publication Data

Library of Congress Control Number: 2022932736

Printed in the United States of America

22 23 24 25 26 LSC 10 9 8 7 6 5 4 3 2 1

We dedicate this book to Tyler Adam Day.
Brother, at all costs,
I'll See You Tomorrow.

Contents

Foreword

My husband, Keith, and I were a disaster waiting to happen. We were each in rational, compatible relationships when we met our junior year of college and instantly dropped those relationships like a pair of hot coals. Keith and I had exactly zero in common except a lot of baggage from childhood. Well, that's not true. We both liked to dance. Our friends tagged us the couple least likely to succeed, and, fourteen months from the day we met, our parents came just short of wearing black to our wedding, making no bones about preferring our previous love interests. I'd been told I'd need surgery to ever conceive a child, but maybe God knew we'd need a seven-pound, three-ounce reason to second-think splitting up. Our first child arrived not quite ten months after the day we married.

Keith and I saw nothing the same way. If he said, "Looks like rain today," I said, "I guess I better turn the sprinkler on the flower bed." If, come Sunday morning, I said, "What a beautiful day for church," he said, "This is perfect fishin' weather" and out he'd go. We drove one another nuts. About four years in and another child later, I'd had enough of marriage and decided to pack a suitcase for my two daughters and me and move in with my parents in a Texas town two hours away.

"I'm leaving Keith," I declared to my best friend on the phone right after Keith pulled out of the driveway for work one morning.

"Okay," she'd said, "Well, come by on your way out of town to say bye and we'll have a quick cup of coffee."

My best friend, three years my senior, lived five minutes from me, so it wasn't out of my way and goodness knows I was going to miss her a heap more than I was going to miss Keith. She had two little boys the same age as my girls, so after walking through the front door, we pitched our kids a bag of Goldfish crackers, sent them off to play, and sat down for coffee.

"Tell me what happened," she said, so I did. Same old stuff, really. We just don't get along. Can't agree on the color of water.

She nodded and kept pouring coffee. Then she baked cookies. Then it was just about lunchtime and she had the stuff to make chicken salad, so why not? I'd leave right after lunch, and the girls would nap all the way to my parents' house. By the time we swallowed our chicken salad, the four kids were in front of a Disney movie and not willing to budge.

"Oh, let 'em watch and I'll make us one more pot of coffee," my friend said.

By the time we had that last drop, it was late afternoon. "Well," I said, "I better get going. Keith will be home soon, and I need to throw on some supper."

"Sounds good!" she said. "I'll see you tomorrow!"

"See you tomorrow!"

That evening Keith asked me how my day had gone. "Fine," I said but thought under my breath, *I left you today, but you don't even know it.*

My best friend and I did this whole routine three or four rounds in those early years, and I fell for it every time. I'd leave

Keith and go as far as her house. She'd fix coffee and let me talk the day away. Let me talk the anger away. Come late afternoon, I'd holler at the girls, "Clean up the toys and let's head to the car. Gotta go fix Dad some dinner!" Best friend of my life. She lives many miles from me now but, by the time she moved, we were in the throes of middle age and I wasn't quite as inclined to leave Keith, especially with the grandkids coming. I figured I'd wait another year. Every December 30 when my wedding anniversary rolls around, I send that same best friend a message that essentially says, "We three—you, Keith, and me—made it another year. Here's to thirty more cups of coffee. God knows I'll likely need them. Thank you, my forever friend. I love you."

That's the beauty of friendship, isn't it? When one lacks resilience, maybe the other's got it to spare. The book you hold in your hands is about building relational resilience when we want to quit. Has that ever been you? It certainly was me, and not only in marriage. I'm currently partnering to build back a few relationships that got splintered in the last decade's divisive cultural and political climate. Maybe we needed a little breathing space for a while in order to let some things cool off, but, this side of it all, a few of us decided some of those differences weren't worth losing good relationships over. After all, relationships—all sorts—are what make the world go around. This book speaks into what keeps our worlds turning, socially speaking. And spiritually speaking. Now I'll share with you how I came to write this foreword.

I had to stop making snap judgments about my entire relationship with someone because of a single incident. Does one night of feeling left out cancel dozens of being brought in?

This was the kind of insight that first drew my attention to

Heather Thompson Day. In all the noise of social media, she has one of those voices that makes me want to quiet down and listen. In a culture polarized by extremes, Heather possesses a gift of nuance that seems near extinction and has the courage to communicate cohesive compassion in a medium committed to misunderstanding. In an age of echo chambers, she's a woman who can think for herself. Heather has got that gorgeous mix: she's vulnerable, but nobody's fool. She's transparent, but not self-indulgent. She can lament and laugh with equal passion. And have I mentioned that Heather's just refreshingly reasonable? It's hard to miss a reasonable person in the craziness of this era. If she gets the idea someone thinks she has a perfect life, she'll burst out laughing and kindly set them straight. I love these things about Heather.

Early on in my exposure to Heather, I noticed how willing she was to be vulnerable if it helped others feel less alone. Lots of people, particularly leaders, talk like they care, but over time I got the distinct impression it wasn't just talk with Heather. She really does care. She wants people to make it. Wants people to know their worth in the eyes of their Maker and the gifts they've been given through Christ even through their pain. She wants them to know when and how to let go and when and how to hang on. She comes alongside people to help them learn how to recognize God-given opportunities and brave the risks in order to find their calling.

When I learned Heather was a communications professor, I smiled to myself and nodded. "Of course she is. Of course she's a teacher." I'd seen it over and over in her, and now it made perfect sense: Heather has a God-given gift of helping people connect and comprehend one another better. She's part interpreter, suggesting that maybe we who are at odds would not dislike each other nearly as much if we simply knew how to communicate. She says maybe we share the same fears but express them in different ways. And she gives hope. Here's an example from these pages,

> "There is life to be lived from right where you are. There is promise available to us right in our present. That is the beauty of still being alive. The story twists at the flip of a page. In one small, otherwise ordinary moment, a seed can be planted that changes everything."

If you're meeting Heather for the first time, it won't take long for you to discover that she's smart, articulate, and relatable. She loves Jesus, loves people, and loves Scripture, and possesses a wisdom beyond her years. In the words of James, a wisdom from above that "is first pure, then peaceable, gentle, open to reason, full of mercy and good fruits, impartial and sincere" (James 3:17–18). That's Heather. I think you're going to love her.

I knew going into this book I'd learn volumes from Heather. She speaks the languages of my learning styles. What I didn't anticipate was all I'd gain from her husband, Seth. Prior to these pages, the only exposure I'd had to Seth was through Heather's writing. Several chapters into the book, I was leaning forward, face inches from the page, with my eyebrows raised. I can tell you in advance there's nothing supplemental about Seth's cowriting. He scoots up a chair of equal size and brings equal insight to the table and, to our tremendous benefit, from such a different perspective and personality that you know both voices are essential to the message. I marked, starred, and underlined one author as much as the other. At one point, Seth asks this question: "What if you are so stuck on what wasn't ideal that you miss what is still possible?"

I measure a good writer by how long it takes to unravel his or her words. You'll think for days about some of the paragraphs Seth has written in this book. One of them describing his childhood introduction to church will stick with me for a long time. Here's just a taste of it:

> "I know how to be a dad because of my mom. . . . Faith for me wasn't a man in a pulpit; it was a woman getting three kids dressed and using her last five dollars for gas."

You're holding gold in your hands, reader. *I'll See You Tomorrow* is not only a great book. It's a great help and so timely and on target that you know God is in it. Go find Him. He's waiting for you.

Beth Moore, President of Living Proof
Ministries, author, and Bible teacher

Introduction

Dear Reader:

There are two sides to everyone we meet. There is the side they present us with, which is typically their best side. Generally, it's their confident side. Their charming side. Their inquisitive side. Their friendly side. Their outgoing side. Their "has it all together" side. But what we see of the people we interact with every day may not be entirely who they are. When they hit the punch card and go home, the person we see at the workplace or at church may have a completely different side. It's their lonely side. Their bitter side. Their unconfident side. Their awkward side. Their depressed side. Their disappointed side. Their unforgiving side. Their triggered side. Their hurt side. It's the side they don't post about because no one would click "Like" on it.

How do I (Seth) know this? Because I have two sides. I have the side that has gotten so used to saying the right words but struggles with how to live up to them. I have the side that truly, genuinely cares about people and yet also doesn't trust them. I know what I want: a life with a community I care about. But the reality is that with relationship comes vulnerability, which means a "willingness to show emotion or to allow one's weakness to be seen or known; willingness to risk being emotionally hurt,"[1] and to be honest, I rarely feel risky. Do you?

It's not hard knowing what to do. It's hard for us to do it. Here's the thing: for years you've probably known what needs to change in your life, but knowing something and doing something are often what separates most of us. We know we need to go to the gym, but how many of us do it? We know we should probably talk to someone about our anxiety, and we will get to it *next week*. I've had a card for a therapist's office in my wallet for over a year. Why do I never actually make the appointment? We know we want to prioritize God. Spend more time with family. Update our résumés. Call that old friend from high school. Finish the book we began reading. We know what we are supposed to do. But how is it that only some people actually do it? If we could just close the gap between today and all we should do tomorrow, our entire lives could look completely different.

I didn't graduate college until after I had two of my three kids. They came to my graduation. For years I knew I wanted to go back to school, but I didn't know how to do it until I looked at my children. That's what loving relationships will do for us. They will provide the *how* to what we already know. What if the purpose to our lives is simply to care about someone else's? What if the only thing more fulfilling than doing it alone is doing it together?

My wife, Heather, and I couldn't be more different. While we were writing this book, I tweeted:

My wife's writing process: Candle burning. Cup of tea.
Total elegance. Single tear streams down her cheek.
    My writing process: Adderall. Red Bull. Music
blasting. Empty cookie carton. Slight feelings of rage as
I access past trauma. Pacing.
    Are . . . are we unequally yoked . . . ?

In this book we won't just give you two perspectives. We
will also give you our two sides. The side we are still working
toward and the reality of where we are. Heather will tell you
what tomorrow can look like. I will be honest with you about
today. I am awkward and shy in large gatherings, but Heather
flourishes. I prefer solitude. Heather seems to finish anything
she starts. I want to quit before I start most things. Heather
is carefree and will strike up a conversation with a stranger
over breakfast. I sip my coffee quietly while scanning for anything that looks out of the ordinary. Heather is social. I am
skeptical. I am a former pastor and campus chaplain. Heather
is a communications professor who has spent the last decade
studying how we can enhance our relationships. I've spent
the last ten years trying to figure out how to even have one.

    Heather is quick to shout from the sideline, "Get back up!"
I will whisper in your ear, "It's okay to stay down."

    We share from two different experiences because we've
lived two very different lives. She's my wife, my better half,
but she's also my opposite. In our ministry we have always
been each other's greatest complement. We will speak to your
pain and your brain. Together, we will encourage your present and your future. If you naturally identify with Heather,
I am going to challenge you to get uncomfortable with other

people's pain. Likewise, if you instinctively gravitate toward me, I invite you to find your inner Heather. What if our two sides are what make us real people? What if confidence would be a detriment without some insecurity? What if risk would be a danger without some healthy fear? What if you aren't two different people? What if you are balancing two sides of what makes us all human?

I will tell you what happens when trust gets broken. Heather will help you pick up the pieces. Every Seth needs a Heather. Every person deserves one cheerleader. And, yes, we could have written this book individually. Each of us sharing from our own perspectives. But we realized it would have only been half of a book. Part of the story. One piece of a reality that is incomplete. When Heather wanted to write about how relationships can save us, I replied, "If only it were that easy."

It is not always that easy. No one knows that more than I.

In every person are two sides. In these pages you'll be safe to bring both of yours. There is an implied promise in the word *tomorrow*. It means there is more than you can see today. So whether you keep community at arm's length or have dozens of friends at the tip of your fingers, there is a promise in this book for both the socialite and the skeptic. What if there is more to your life than what you can see today? What if the night eventually gives way to morning? What if there is a bigger picture to all of us than any single mirror can reveal? But I can't prove all this in just an introduction.

Which is why *I'll see you tomorrow.*

Your friend,

Seth

CHAPTER 1

Loving Yourself So You Can Love Others

The greatest weapon against stress is our ability to choose one thought over another.
WILLIAM JAMES

"I quit."

It was almost midnight. I (Heather) was sitting at the back of the bus, riding home after my final track meet of the season. I placed my hood over my head and hoped it would signal to those around me that I didn't want to talk. Tears streamed down my cheeks. My entire life up until this point revolved around becoming a college athlete. And I had done that. I had a scholarship to run track at a small Christian college in Indiana. But nothing had gone as planned.

There were so many nights I sobbed in my dorm and was

asked "Can you be quiet?" by my roommates. God bless their ministry.

So because I was nineteen and dramatic, I picked up the phone and called the only person I knew who would answer my call at midnight and then do something totally irrational: my mother. Takes one to know one.

"Please, come get me," I whispered into the phone.

I didn't want to spend another minute on that campus. I have never felt more misunderstood than I did my freshman year of college. Maybe that is why I am the type of college professor I am today. I don't want to just teach students; I want to serve them. I serve them where I often felt most hurt. When a college freshman cries in my office, I don't roll my eyes. I know what those tears feel like. If you want to know where God may be calling you, look back. What gaps did you fall in? How can you fill them so someone else doesn't? I didn't have many friends my freshmen year. Not true, meaningful friendships. I had some great teammates. I met some precious people. But I rarely felt like anyone there fully understood me.

One time in college my friends and I went to Red Lobster. We dressed up and I thought it would be like the movies, where we laugh so hard we cry and then go back to campus and share our deepest, darkest, and crap. I wanted to bond. I had been expelled from my last Christian school experience in middle school, and so I intentionally chose a Christian college where I could try my hand at a do-over. Jesus said to love one another and build his church, and I desperately wanted to do that. I was so loved at my secular high school. My friends weren't Christians, but they gave me community. They let me belong. They made me feel safe. Maybe that's why I teach at a Christian university. I want to stand in the gap of the kid who would never feel worthy enough to lead a chapel.

It's similar to what Charles Wesley wrote in a hymn: "I the chief of sinners am, but Jesus dy'd for me!"[1]

Halfway through dinner I realized this was a coup. The girl down the hall started screaming that this wasn't my small-town high school and I wasn't queen bee. (First of all, babe, this wasn't Harvard. This was small-town Indiana, so let's all just relax.) I was outmanned and outnumbered. I shoved a cheddar biscuit into my mouth and swallowed my pride. This wasn't my first rodeo. In my Christian elementary school there was an I Hate Heather Club. Thank God my husband, Seth, never joined. My relationship with Seth is unique. He is not just my husband. He has always been my best friend. He is the person who gets me. Even in sixth grade, before Seth loved me, he liked me. When other kids said I was "too much," he said they were jealous. When I was told by a teacher I was too loud, he would whisper, "You're hilarious." Some of my fondest memories are being eleven and jumping on my trampoline outside with Seth laughing and shouting and repeating lines from movies we didn't even understand. Seth calls me out on my stuff, but he also reminds me of my potential. I was lucky, at age eleven, to have a friend like him.

When people say adult friendships are hard, I say amen. Except for a handful of people, every deeply meaningful relationship I have is with people who have known me since I was navigating the I Hate Heather Club. I guess friendship is forged in foxholes. There are very few people from my college days at either university I attended that are a part of my daily life. I was told I'd make my best friends in college. If that's true, I'm screwed. But I have learned how to make a couple of truly vital adult relationships with people who let me fill in all our blanks. We don't need a sorority. But we do need relationship. We need genuine people in our corner that we pledge allegiance to. Whatever you hate about your life right now, whatever darkness you can't see through, whatever painful church experience, toxic job culture, or family dinner you can't see yourself on the other side of, there is another side. Pain and praise. That's our lives. There is praise on the other side of your pain. But when we are still in pain, it is hard to see that.

"Please, come get me," I whispered into the phone that night, and then held my breath as I waited to hear what my mother would say.

And so, at 2:00 a.m. on a small Indiana campus, my mommy came and got me. Together, we collected everything I had brought with me to college—my dreams and my clothes—and put them in the back of her Chevrolet. We drove home. Here I was, doing the only thing I wanted to do my entire life—run track—and yet I quit after my freshman year. I quit what I loved, not because of what I was doing but because of who I was with. I emailed my truly fantastic coaches and told them I wouldn't be back the next school year. Sometimes I'll see some of the few relationships I made that year pop up on my Instagram and I smile. They went on to make more memories at that school, without me. As it turns out, living your dream doesn't really matter. Not if you feel alone.

This is the problem with living in situations where we don't feel loved or even liked, and especially when we don't feel safe. It robs us of joy. It is hard to see what's good when our relationships are bad. When we don't feel safe, our brain spends a lot of energy focusing on potential threats. And, dear one, you have only so much energy, and there are oh, so many threats, even if we aren't in the middle of a coup at a Red Lobster.

When we don't feel safe at church, we don't want to serve. When we don't feel safe at work, we want to quit. When we don't feel safe in our country, we aren't sure how much we want to contribute to it. When we don't feel safe in our marriage, we have no place that feels like home. And when we don't feel safe with our family, holidays aren't holy. On Abraham Maslow's hierarchy of needs, right after food and water, is safety.[2] Food, water, and safety. Only after we feel safe can we look for ways to belong. When people don't feel like they belong in our churches, maybe it isn't because they hate religion. Maybe they are leaving what hasn't made them feel safe. And, beloved, that's on us, not them.

When we feel safe we can spend the energy we aren't wasting calculating potential threats on thinking of creative ways to be even more productive. We take risks when we feel safe to take them. We look for how we can belong to our organizations and what loving ways we can serve our churches. We will even put in more work at our jobs. But when we must watch our backs as well as our fronts, our eyes get tired.

I tweeted the other day, "Do we hate our lives? Or are we just really really tired?"

And one person responded, "The fact that I can't answer this question tells me all I need to know." Sound familiar?

What if we *don't* actually hate our lives? What if we are just really, really tired? I am a professor of communication at Andrews University, and I believe the single biggest predictor to how well you feel your life is going right now is not what you are doing but who you are with. When we don't have healthy, positive relationships with others, we make rash decisions at 2:00

a.m. We are more likely to quit even the things we love. We don't see the track. We see the bus ride home. We don't see the scholarship. We see tears and cheddar biscuits. When you don't have people to hold you, you end up holding yourself.

Researchers at Carnegie Mellon University found that what makes us thrive is having relationships. They concluded, "Past research has shown that individuals with supportive and rewarding relationships have better mental health, higher levels of subjective well-being and lower rates of morbidity and mortality."[3]

The Fraying

It is very difficult for me to cancel work but oddly much easier for me to cancel people. I think part of that is because I am already under so much stress in my career and family life (thank you, pandemic) that a single error on part of a friendship makes the whole relationship feel more draining than it was. Some of what I have felt were draining relationships were simply my entering relationships drained. It is hard to give what we don't have. So job, church, friends, family, whatever you want from me, I probably don't have anything left.

One time I called a friend for advice because I was experiencing some relational drain. I have only so many close relationships. The people I am close to, I am extremely close to. Five of my six deepest relationships are with people I have known for a minimum of ten years.

My sister Natasha was never the type of older sister who is embarrassed to be around her younger sibling. When her friends came over, she would tell everyone to sit down, because they just had to listen to me tell this hilarious story. If there was ever a day in my life I doubted that God had a plan for me, my sister would set me straight. I can remember being eight years old and her telling me I was special. So if the girl down my college hall-way was wondering why my self-esteem was so high, she could blame Natasha.

My best friend, Scarlett, and I have been friends for nearly two decades. And she's been there for it all. When I was six-teen, I got my driver's license. I picked up Scarlett, who was still fifteen at the time, and we headed to the nearest quality dining experience. Thirty minutes later we strolled into a TGI Fridays with enough savings to fund our own meals. I ordered steak skewers. When we were finished, I asked for a to-go box for my leftovers.

"Oh, darn," I said. "I don't have any steak sauce at home, so this won't be as good when I eat it later."

I went to the bathroom before coming back to the table to meet Scarlett and collect my belongings. As we headed to the car, I noticed she was walking funny.

"What's wrong with you?" I asked her as she beelined for the door.

"Here," she said as we got outside. There, in the broad sun-light, my best friend reached down her pants and removed a half-used bottle of steak sauce.

"You shoved steak sauce down your pants?" I asked her confused.

"Yes," she said nonchalantly. "For your leftovers."

We both erupted in laughter. I can still see us in my mind, with tears coming down my face as I clutched this bottle of steak sauce my best friend had just lifted from a TGI Fridays. She was willing to get a misdemeanor for the sake of my leftovers, and I had never felt more loved. To this day there is not a girls' weekend Scarlett and I spend together that I don't bring up the image of her hobbling out of that restaurant with a bottle of sauce down her pant leg. I am laughing even as I write this.

I understand you may be judging us. We were teenagers. We were stupid. I assure you I have done far more offensive stuff than eat the sauce from my friend's denim. I do not condone theft. I stole an ankle bracelet at thirteen, and it broke when I went to put it on in the car. I hadn't even left the parking lot. I never stole anything again. I knew for a fact that God had just struck that Jezebel medallion. I went home and read from the book of Isaiah—"In that day the Lord will take away the finery of the anklets, the headbands, and the crescents; the pendants, the bracelets, and the scarves" (3:18–19 ESV)—and I prayed for forgiveness. Even confessed to my parents. Three dollars and ninety-nine cents was not worth my soul, and I left my life of petty theft behind. Hallelujah!

I tell you this story to illustrate the longevity of some of my friendships. Sure, these women may look put together now in their nice houses and with their fancy titles, but I know where they came from. I know where the bodies are buried. Casual friendships are one thing, but some of the people I call friends are people with whom I share a long, complex history. My friend Jewel is someone I have been friends with since the third grade. We were both expelled from our Christian middle schools on the same day (as I told you, the steak sauce is the least of your worries). She knows me probably as well as my own sister does.

My friend Vimbo I met at summer camp. I was nineteen.

She was fifteen. Today, she is thirty-one. For over fifteen years she has been the collector of my secrets, the giver of my hope, and the protector of my peace. My friend Cortney I have known since I was twenty-two. We are nothing alike politically. I wouldn't watch the news with her if my life depended on it. But we are both so much more than who we vote for. She is truly one of the sincerest women I have ever met. I would trust her with my life. I love her like she shares my bloodline. It's going to take more than politics to separate her from me, although I would like to give her my reading list.

My friend Tiffany is my newest relationship, but what we haven't experienced in years we have more than made up for in hardship. We met when both of us were at the most difficult season of our adult lives. My spirit recognized her instantly, and I knew beyond a doubt that God had sent me someone who would make me feel at home though the place I was living was not my home. If I was throwing a birthday party for myself that first year I lived in Denver, Tiffany would have been the first name I put on my list. And if I am being honest, I would have struggled to come up with many more. I was surrounded by people and yet I had very few people. My desire for you at the end of this book is to be able to put names on your list. This year we are going to throw ourselves a birthday party, and by the end of this book, our goal is to have the confidence to write more than a single name. This year we are going to stand back up. But not by our sheer will and self-reliance. Self-reliance is a myth.

Relationships are crucial. They are a fundamental. They are literally what gives our lives meaning and purpose. We can survive our darkest days when we stay connected with our dearest people. And yet when I am overworked and underpaid, when I am against deadlines and swim lessons, when my dad's health is poor and my finances are tight, it is easy for me to enter even these most intimate relationships feeling strained.

Recently, I was drained and saw something a friend had said that really offended me. I remember the second I read it my face got hot. Being stabbed in the back is deadly, but what cuts more deeply is being stabbed from the front. *Was I being dramatic? Was I reading this incorrectly? Why would she say that?* Have you ever had one of those moments where it takes your brain a second to catch up with what happened? And so you just stand somewhere getting mental error codes because it doesn't add up, and your brain struggles to make sense of it at all. It was like watching your grandma use her iPhone—could not compute. That's where I was emotionally, and so I picked up the phone and called the person who has known me the longest and asked if I was overreacting.

"Oh, no," Jewel said. "You can call her out. You have grounds for that."

See? This is why I called her. Of all my friends, Jewel is probably the quickest to side with me, no questions asked. These are good people to keep around, by the way. If I'm standing, Jewel is standing. If I'm crawling, Jewel is crawling. If I'm going through hell, she is laying down beside me.

"Or—" Wait what? I thought. Are we landing this plane in victim valley or what?

"Or," she continued, "you can look past this single event and choose to see this issue within the scope of your ten-year friendship and just choose to love her beyond this isolated incident."

My spirit clapped within me the second she said it. I didn't even fight it. Jewel was right. My friend was still wrong, and yet Jewel was still right. She has always given solid advice, but this was tweet worthy. I had wanted to stand up for myself. My instinct was to make a big deal of this. I watched a talk show in college once, and I never forgot this one episode where the host said, "People can't walk over you unless you lay down first."

I was ready to march. I was ready to school my other friend on a lesson in loyalty. Let her know that I had boundaries and she had crossed them. I was already frayed, and I was entering a painful situation with very little elastic left. I think that's what happens to us a lot of times. We don't have the mental energy to do the work relationships require, and so we just burn them or mute them or block them. That is much less taxing than making peace with them. Adult friendships are hard because adults are exhausted.

Jewel is a woman I have known since I was nine. I think she may be the only person I could hear saying something like that.

Lesson number one: find your Jewel, be honest with your Jewel, and trust their counsel. I am serious about this. Who are you sharing your internal scripts with? You have to share them. These internal stories we tell ourselves will eat us alive if we don't ever seek outside perspective.

Jewel reminded me that the only way we got from nine years old to thirty-five years old still on each other's recent call list is by not doing isolated incidents. We measure our relationship in the scope of its entirety. I had probably thrown Jewel under the bus at some point in our twenty-five-year run called friendship. I said *probably*, but that's because this is my story. I have absolutely done things to hurt our friendship. I've been the villain in someone else's book. And now I know why Jewel continued to be my friend. Because though we have had incidents, we never had a pattern. Incidents can be forgiven; patterns must be broken.

And yet when it felt as if I were the rightful victim, I was quick to forget what all my friends had probably already done for me. So much of life is just deciding when to say something. And then regretting what we said, or what we didn't. This time, I don't regret it. I didn't say anything. I didn't march. I didn't call her out. I didn't subtweet or give a lecture. I just let it go. And I am so glad I did. Because there hasn't been another isolated incident with that friend yet.

Sometimes we all screw up. Sometimes we are all a bad friend to someone. Sometimes we let jealousy override our empathy. Sometimes we don't invite others when we should have. Sometimes we are human beings filled with errors. Sometimes we are trying to make ourselves feel like the kingpin or queen bee. A series of incidents—maybe I am just a bad friend. But one? Should we define anyone by one single choice? Maybe, depending on how awful that choice was. But not always.

Today, I know the value of being thirty-five years old and still being able to call my friend from third grade. I know what it feels like to have my brain not be able to process someone's betrayal. But I also have known loyalty. The scale can't tip only toward the negative. I must also weigh the positives. It's priceless. Jewel knows me. She gets me. She knows when what someone else says about me is true and when it's totally uncalled for. She is one of my favorite people to process with simply because she has seen me in so many different situations. And you don't get to that point without laying down a time or two in between.

It's okay to end relationships. Sometimes we may have to. But I do wonder if, in our quickness to protect ourselves, we haven't lost something greater. The ability to have friendships and romantic relationships and jobs that span decades. No one gets to year ten without having some drama in between. We need each other. In fact, I don't think we will survive this season without finding a team we can lean fully into. The good, the bad, the ugly. What we can't do alone, we can do together. So what if, instead of always saying goodbye, we started saying, "I'm going to process this. I need some space to think it through. I'm hurt and I need to walk away right now. But *I'll see you tomorrow.*" There is an implicit promise in the word *tomorrow*. It means that life has pages, and pages don't determine endings. Some experiences are for a season, but hope belongs to the morning.

I'm Fine

I was alone in a hotel room. It was almost midnight. The air was humid and the decor hadn't been updated in decades. The room was so quiet. No loud partygoers were frequenting this small town, even though summer held its most popular months. It was a Chautauqua formed in 1873 by members of the Methodist Church. I had bad cell service—I think they do that intentionally. It was the kind of place you go to reconnect with God and find yourself.

Here I was, finding myself. Or maybe I was losing myself? If you read my last book, *It's Not Your Turn*, you know already that sometimes it takes being lost to realize how deeply you need to be found. I can hardly provide words to express how scared I was. My entire abdomen tightened suddenly. I felt there should be a warning before your body gives that kind of siren. I wanted to cry, but the pain was so intense my eyes couldn't make tears. *God help me*, I whispered over and over. *What is happening to me?*

My stomach felt as if it was actually twisting. *Which side is my appendix?* I wondered. It was as if someone with burly hands were wringing my insides, and the more I gasped, the harder they squeezed. I have given birth three times, and the intensity in my gut was on the same playing field as what I experienced then. Except I wasn't pregnant, and I didn't know what was happening.

God help me, I whispered.

I was in the middle of speaking for a weeklong teen evangelistic series in Lakeside, Ohio. I had seen God move in powerful ways and started to genuinely worry I was being physically attacked by the devil.

God help me, I repeated.

This felt like torment, and I was considering calling for an ambulance. But, instead, I picked up the phone and called my mentor, Jose Rojas. It was late and this was inappropriate, but I wasn't sure who else would know if I was amid some type of supernatural spiritual warfare. I had never seen *The Blair Witch Project*. My parents didn't even let me watch the Harry Potter movies. I was a sitting duck.

Jose answered the phone, and I choked out what was going on inside this little hotel room near Lake Erie.

"You are not being attacked by the devil," he said calmly. "You are being attacked by yourself."

"Are you sure? Because I feel like I should call for a medical evaluation," I said through a clenched jaw.

I was hoping he would bring some anointing oil. A crucifix might be a bit much, but I'd never been in this situation before, so it was probably best to have all hands on deck. I was pretty sure Lucifer himself was about to run up my ceiling. I'm a Protestant, but I was open to a jar of holy water if it meant the twisting feeling in my intestines would go down to a level seven out of ten.

"I have been hospitalized with your same symptoms at least three times before," he said in a very low, calm voice that clearly wasn't picking up the 911 urgency of my current situation.

"The Lord is near, but you are a human being. And your body is reacting to the stress you're under," he said.

"I'm not stressed," I responded.

"Stress often has no warnings, Heather. It will just sit in your system patiently until your body breaks beneath it. It should pass within an hour. I have had episodes that lasted days. But if this is your first time, you should notice it gradually lighten."

As he was talking, I noticed I was no longer in complete agony. My body was still curled into a ball, but more so in a defensive position. I looked at the clock. Seventy-five minutes had passed. I was still in pain, but we could hold off on any surgery. Still, I was open to a Xanax.

He prayed with me and repeated some scriptures. My mentor is so wise. I often race to my prayer journal to write down the little gems he passes out so I won't forget them. He is a walking fortune cookie.

"Listen to your body," he said before leaving me with his parting words that I have never forgotten. "And eat some papaya."

This was the first time I felt my body physically buckle under the stress I was putting on myself. Since then I have read countless articles and watched several YouTube videos about people experiencing physical symptoms due to acute stress. Apparently, there is a powerful connection between our guts and our brains. In fact, the part of your body that contains the largest area of nerves, outside of your brain, is your gut, and there are shared nerve connections between your digestive tract and your brain.[4] I wasn't being tortured by demons (classic Christian leap, though, am I right?). I was stressed and needed to eat some papaya, which, by the way, is traditionally used to treat ulcers. Papain is a natural digestive enzyme in papaya that helps the body to process foods that could otherwise be contributing to irritating the stomach lining.[5] I'll move on since this isn't a health food guide, but I know that was a whole sermon for someone.

I didn't even know I was stressed. I was *fine*. I had just finished defending my dissertation a few months earlier. I had been at optimal functioning up until the moment I wasn't. That same day I had preached two sermons, submitted a *Newsweek* article back to my editor, and negotiated some logistics with my new employer as I prepared to move across the country. I had put the finishing touches on a book proposal, in between telling seventeen-year-old kids at a Christian summer camp that their relationship with God was about more than their sexual purity. See? I wasn't stressed. I was *fine*. Sure, life was a bit chaotic that summer, but I didn't have time to focus on any of that.

I mean, yeah, that may be a lot for most people, but not for me. I am a pusher. That's what I do. I push through. I am resilient. I am self-reliant. I put the car in Drive and get to the destination. I have no idea why my gut decided to turn on me like this, because I am a strong, independent person who is not stressed (stop me when I'm getting warm). I was *fine*. I had mastered the art of driving seventy miles an hour on a freeway while air slowly seeps out of all four of my tires. This was no biggie. I'm the strong friend. I'm the one you call at 2:00 a.m. when you are ready to leave your toxic relationship. I throw open the passenger-side door and tell you to get into the car. We are riding on rims and have a cracked windshield, but where there is a will there is a way, baby! I am not the unstable person with a physical manifestation of a deeper mental issue. I was *fine*. And yet here I was, with my airbags deployed and my gas tank on *E* in the middle of an evangelistic series that was about to come to a screeching halt. I was *not* fine.

I called the event organizers in the morning and told them I had to reduce my schedule. I sat in shame and gnawed on papaya in my empty hotel room while thinking a demon would have made for a better story. At this point I'd take Casper the Friendly Ghost if it meant I could shift some of this blame. But I had done this to myself. I was the lunatic driving the car. My self-reliance could be the death of me.

My refusal to slow down, my objections to acknowledging where I was hurt, my need to be the steady hand in every room are the very things that debilitated me. The problem with always being the strong friend is that, after you have carried everyone else to safety, who is left to carry you? No one dives in for the lifeguard. Part of being a strong swimmer is knowing when to float. I'd like you to take some time with Seth and me and to float for a bit. Let's slow down and assess the damage. Let's take stock of where we are today before we go chasing tomorrow. What if we have to love ourselves in order to love each other? What if empty glasses can't fill other people's jars? What if none of us are meant to be self-reliant?

· · · ·

This book contains twelve chapters, and I'd like you to join us for each of them. I don't want you to miss anything, because each concept will build on the next as we discover that not only do we need to learn to love each other but we also need to remember to love ourselves. This book is about hope, and as you read it, we have included questions at the end of each chapter for you to engage deeper with yourself and, if possible, someone else.

As you continue, I would like to challenge you with this quote from bell hooks in an interview she did with Maya Angelou in 1998. She said of reading, "For most people, what is so painful about reading is that you read something and you don't have anybody to share it with. In part what the book club opens up is that people can read a book and then have someone else to talk about it with. Then they see that a book can lead to the pleasure of conversation, that the solitary act of reading can actually be a part of the path to communion and community."[6]

I purposely invited Seth to write this book with me because I knew it would be incomplete if he didn't. I didn't want to write a book about relational community alone. That defeats my very purpose. I believe we are better together and not just figuratively. How can I tell you how to get back up if we don't explore why people fall? I didn't write this book with Seth because he is my husband. This is not a marriage book. I asked him to write it with me because he is the one who taught me that not everything can be pushed through. Seth has taught me to listen before I talk. He has challenged me to give reverence to people's pain.

I would say, "We have to keep moving," and Seth would say, "Not until we acknowledge why our bodies are standing still."

I am so honored to pen words beside him because he is so deeply reflective, so acutely attentive, and so preciously committed to Christ, despite never having an easy hand. My relationship with Seth has made me a better human being. I have no doubt that writing with him will give us a better book and a more realistic and complete story, because that is what relationships offer us: wholeness. This book is about assessing the damage of where you are today so you can keep believing in tomorrow. I would have just focused on tomorrow. Seth reminded me that some of us can't see past today. What if, just as this book would have been incomplete without Seth's perspective, our lives are incomplete without a relational view? What if our churches are only as honest as our diversity? What if our politics are only as practical as the varying demographics that engage them? What if we can't have all the answers on our own? What if questions are a vital part of how we can better connect to ourselves and with each other? What if the greatest stories allow for more than one narrative? The first step of Alcoholics Anonymous is admitting you have a problem. And, oh, Houston, do we have a problem!

We have a "push" problem. The myth of self-reliance is going to destroy us from the inside out. The ideal of American success and fortitude is that we grit our teeth and claw our way back to the top. If you get knocked down, then you must stand back up. But does anyone know what they are standing for anymore? For money? For independence? For followers? What are we standing for? We aren't just working for the weekend; we are working for the vacation. We glorify stories of people who sacrifice everything to claw and crawl their way to independence. But what if humans weren't meant to live independent of one another? What if the most holistic sense of individuality is created by deeper community? I don't want you to crawl. Not today. Today, I want to lay down beside you.

Our lives weren't meant to be pushed through. You can't push through divorce. You can't push through insecurity. You can't push through grief. You can't push through stress. If our goal in life is to somehow find peace, we must stop pushing. You can't push toward peace. The very definition of peace is freedom from disturbance.[7] Sometimes that disturbance is our need to fix it or our need to find something to alleviate the pain we are experiencing. Trying to push your way toward peace will always cause you to push right past it.

What if peace isn't something we find but rather something we let find us? When we stop disturbing all the water with our flailing arms and pumping legs, we let ourselves rise to the surface. The sun glows on our skin and we lie in a bed of blue and just breathe there for a while. A light breeze. No waves. No more disturbance. The water fills our ears so we can't hear anything. Our eyes lock onto a few clouds and we just rest peacefully in it all. What if peace is something that can be experienced only when we finally surrender? What if standing alone isn't what human beings were created to do? What if we were meant to stand together? What if brotherhood and sisterhood is worth standing back up for?

"The Lord is near," my mentor said, "but you are a human being, and your body is reacting to the stress you're under."

• • • •

I read something Michael Jordan, arguably the greatest basketball player to ever play, said about how he handles high-pressure games. "The only way to relieve that pressure is to build your fundamentals, practice them over and over, so when the game breaks down, you can handle anything that transpires."[8]

What are our fundamentals? What are the basics that

we know to be true without having to think? What if we practiced those even in times of ease so that, when the game breaks down, we can handle anything that transpires? I think what God showed me during that week in Ohio was that in tandem with the ministry of presence is the ministry of our own absence. It is a healthy thing to know that God will still be God without me. That should be a fundamental. Our absence is a reminder to ourselves and others that we are, in fact, not God. That God wants us to co-labor, but with four tires and a tank of gas. Our exhaustion is not evangelism, and our hurry isn't holy. In fact, we worship a God who commands our rest and therefore commands our absence. Rest should be a fundamental habit of the Christian spirit. We must take a day off.

"Remember the sabbath day," the Lord wrote with his own finger, "to keep it holy" (Ex. 20:8 KJV). Your rest is holy. Your peace has a purpose. Your absence is a ministry. God never asked you to be the steady hand in every room.

God says, "My own hand laid the foundations of the earth, and my right hand spread out the heavens" (Isa. 48:13). I'm sorry, but do you see *your* hand in the text?

Job says, "Which of all these does not know that the hand of the LORD has done this? In his hand is the life of every creature and the breath of all mankind" (12:9–10).

The Lord says, "Do not fear, for I am with you; do not be dismayed, for I am your God. I will strengthen you and help you; I will uphold you with my righteous right hand" (Isa. 41:10).

Put your little, shaky, approval-seeking hand down. Stick it in your pocket and let it rest awhile. Your hand is not what is important here. It is the hand of God that saves. The Lord is near. But you are a human being, and your body will react to the stress you put it under.

I'll See You Tomorrow

All around us, the world is breaking. Piece by piece, person by person, each of us is struggling to figure out how to survive today. My students say to me, "I am one small push or unkind word away from totally self-destructing," and if I am honest, on many days, so am I. Life feels like one giant off-season. It feels like all I see is loss at every corner. I'm trying to do everything I can to not let my body break beneath the stress it's under. And it is on days like these that Michael Jordan said we must remember the fundamentals. What have you decided is a fundamental?

In the documentary series *The Last Dance* that chronicles the history of Michael Jordan and the Chicago Bulls, Tim Grover, who spent fifteen years as Michael's personal trainer, tells the story in episode eight of when Jordan lost to the Orlando Magic. The team felt defeated. Tim said that he turned to Jordan as they are walking off the court and said, "Just let me know when I will see you."

It was the off-season. They had lost. It was time to go home and wallow. This chapter had ended.

But Jordan said, "*I'll see you tomorrow*," and walked off the court.

I guess that is why Michael Jordan is Michael Jordan. When everyone else went home, he said, "I'll see you tomorrow."

What if that is what we all need right now? What if today isn't the day for self-improvement? What if today isn't the day to be the steady hand? What if today isn't the time to offer your "fix it" or reconcile all that's been broken? What if today it is okay to lose? Maybe today you lost your job. Maybe today you saw a Christian post something that makes you embarrassed to be one. Maybe today someone abused your goodness. Maybe today you discovered they cheated. Maybe today your child left for what feels like the last time. Maybe today you scared yourself because you thought about how easy it would be to die. What happens today may require us to stop. To lie down. To play dead where we are mid-crawl. But, again, there is an implicit promise in the word *tomorrow*. And I want you to remember that. Today, maybe you can't. So *I'll see you tomorrow*.

I spoke at a conference with Seth Franco. He told the audience that when he was in high school, he had been struggling with depression, and a teacher pulled him aside and said something like, "If you ever have a night you don't think you'll make it through, promise me, you'll give it till tomorrow."

Seth had been an emotional kid who struggled with chronic physical pain. He has hip dysplasia. Like Michael Jordan, he was a fantastic basketball player. He played in college, but the pain in his hip socket made it impossible for him to take his game to the next level. One night as an adult he was at the end of his rope and wanted to take his life, but he remembered the voice of his teacher: "If you ever have a night you don't think you'll make it through, promise me, you'll give it till tomorrow." Her voice came flooding back to him, and moved by the memory, he did just as she said. He didn't take his life. Instead, he fell asleep. The next morning he learned that Universal Studios was filming a movie about basketball in Harlem. Seth Franco didn't know it, but the night he wanted to end his life was the second night of a three-day tryout for the movie. He tried out and was cast for the lead role.[9]

Seth Franco was also the first white player since 1942 to tour with the Harlem Globetrotters. He did eventually have to have surgery on his hip. But while he was in a wheelchair, he spent his time practicing basketball tricks with his hands. He now tours the country and tells kids about faith and challenges. He tells them how what we feel today isn't always what we will feel tomorrow.

"My story is just like a basketball," he says. "You can get pushed down in life, but the harder life pushes you down, the higher you soar."[10]

However, while that can be true, sometimes being pushed down just leaves us on the floor. So if we've been pushed down, let's weep. Today, we can scream. Today, we can call up whoever's left and run through what all went wrong. Today, it may feel like the devil's attacking you. Today may feel like failure. But *I'll see you tomorrow.*

Our world is a rubber band that has been stretched so far that the edges are frayed. We are all one push or one unkind word away from breaking. We are collectively standing at the edge of a cliff and hoping no more ground beneath us wavers. Our hearts can't handle one more thing. *God help me*, we all cry in unison.

My Christian experience so far has been with the God of "daily bread." I haven't met the God of "excess" yet. But I know a lot about the God of little by little. The God of patience. The God of "just enough." In Matthew 6:9–11, when the Lord taught the disciples how to pray, he taught them to say, "Our Father in heaven, hallowed be your name, your kingdom come, your will be done, on earth as it is in heaven. Give us today our daily bread." And that is the God I have known. The God of "daily bread."

If today all you have is enough energy or hope or faith for just this one single day, what if that is all you need? The thing about a God who provides daily bread is that there is more coming tomorrow. When it feels as if we have expended all our resources, thank goodness that the God of yesterday, today, and forever says,

"I'll see you tomorrow."

. . . .

Your right hand, O LORD, glorious in power, your right hand, O LORD, shatters the enemy. (Ex. 15:6 ESV)

ENGAGE

- Today, what are your hopes for tomorrow?
- What was a time you didn't think you'd make it through?
- Share a low moment from your week. What is one area of your life that doesn't feel so fine?

1) Today 10/27/22 - my hopes for
Tomorrow: Healing, peace,
giving of myself to others,
financial freedom - Family,
joy, vacation - Adventure,

2) Sitting in the dark, in my closet
2018

3.) Dealing w/ Mental Health ups & downs
w/ my family

CHAPTER 2

Do What's Possible

It can take years to mold a dream. It takes only a fraction of a second for it to be shattered.

MARY E. PEARSON

"Get off the hood, Cecil!"

Those were the words that my (Seth) mother yelled with her window cracked open just enough to let her words out but not enough to let the crazy man in. The air was thin. My mother was breathing heavily, and the cold seat buckles signaled she was in a rush to make her exit.

Cecil was my father.

It is still difficult for me to call him that. What is a father anyway?

The answer probably looks different for everyone. We make sweeping statements about fathers, though, and people nod their heads because no one wants to be the one to say out loud, "My father wasn't like that." For some kids their father is the man with the briefcase who maybe doesn't talk much but always comes back home at the end of the day.

My dad was the opposite. Lots of empty words, very little time at home. I haven't spoken to Cecil in three years. But you wouldn't know that if you looked at Facebook.

He is the first to comment on a sermon: "That's my boy!"

Still, so many empty words.

My relationship with my father is complicated. I don't have bitterness or anger anymore. I forgive him. I think I even understand him. But in a lot of ways, he is the reason I still struggle so deeply in relationships. It is very difficult for children to trust strangers when the people they know best are so untrustworthy. *Trust* is the hardest word for me to say. Some people choke on *I love you*. My muscles get tense with *I trust you*. Trust takes time and repetition and effort. I think that's why there is so little of it. We are all still recovering from the last time we mustered it.

It's interesting how tiny moments from our past can make such an impact in our present. We go through life every day wondering who we can truly trust.

Should I really give my credit card information to this person over the phone?

Should I tell a friend what I'm struggling with at home?

Should I trust my coworker to know my ideas?

Should I let this person babysit my children?

Is this church safe?

Will these people take whatever piece of myself I give them and extort me with it later?

A lot of our life is deciding who we can trust and making

good instinctual decisions on who we can't. Think about how much energy all of that takes. And for kids who grow up not fully knowing who they can trust in childhood, it can be difficult to learn to trust themselves. It can be difficult to learn how to make decisions that we trust in, because life is filled with uncertainty all the time. As Heather already mentioned, things are only getting more stretched, stressed, and uncertain. How do we deal with it?

Heather jokes that watching me pick my cereal in the morning is painful. I can't make up my mind. Often with even simple choices, such as what I want to eat, my brain doesn't react quickly. It's a symptom of complex trauma.[1] People who experienced reoccurring trauma in childhood struggle with concentration and decision-making. Heather said that stress can impact our brain's ability to handle the everyday pressures life can bring, but past trauma can put stress on steroids. Stress, according to therapist Jamie Marich, is essentially anything that disturbs our balance. She wrote, "In other words, stress is anything life brings our way that has the potential to upset our balance. Thus, traumatic experiences are always stressful, but stressors are not always traumatic."[2]

Most people will experience varying degrees of stress. But some of us will also experience varying degrees of trauma. I certainly have stress in my life, but I've also experienced trauma.

Kathryn Millán gives some examples of what trauma symptoms can look like. I want to share some of them with you in case you are wondering if this relates to your situation.[3] Trauma can cause anxiety, increased irritability and anger, and sleeplessness. You may find yourself often shut down or unable to reach a goal. You may struggle with depression or have a change in appetite or be unable to concentrate.[4] And, yes, I also struggle with these things, but right now we are talking about you. Stay focused.

How it impacts our relationships is that it can make us distrusting of others. We may even avoid our friends and loved ones. We chronically feel unsafe. The thing about trauma is that it doesn't just make us distrust untrustworthy people; it may cause us to distrust even trustworthy people. If you are like me, you may have trouble bonding or being vulnerable with people you have bonded with. It wasn't until graduate school when I studied human service counseling that I started to be able to articulate what I had thought were just my quirks. What if it wasn't just that I was angry? What if I was still healing? Have you ever cut yourself? It hurts if someone touches it. Your skin is healing. People must be gentle. It can also hurt when people trigger our past pain. We are still healing. It's okay to be gentle.

Cecil sitting on the hood of my mom's car is one of my first memories of going to church. He sat on the hood in an effort to control her. He was always trying to do that, even long after she left him. Once he couldn't control her anymore, he tried to control my image of her. Even in adulthood. He would rewrite memories and add himself into them as if he had been there.

A few years ago, he asked if I remembered the time my older brother, Tyler, and I were attacked by bees. He told an elaborate story of carrying us back to my granny's farmhouse and then pulling dozens of stingers out of our bodies.

I remembered what happened. I remembered the stings. But it wasn't Cecil who carried me. It was my mother. She wrapped my brother and me in her arms and ran through a swarm of angry bees until she got us to safety. It was my mother who removed the stingers. Someone must have told him the story later. When he tells it now, though, he has removed my mom and inserted himself as the hero. It's interesting to think about, honestly.

Gripping the sides of the family Ford, he yelled, "If you're going, you're going to have to go with me on the hood of your car!"

This time his words fell flat as my mother glanced behind and looked at each of my brothers and me sitting in the back seat before taking one last look at Cecil. He was still glued to the windshield, trying to obstruct her vision. I thought she would put the car in Park. No place could be this important. But I was wrong. Slowly, putting the car in Reverse, the car started to roll backward. My mother had made a decision that day that I think probably impacted a lot of the decisions she would make for years to come. She was going to church. And nothing was going to stop her.

Cecil's yelling turned to visceral screams as my mom flipped the car into Drive. He was losing control. He was losing her. As she drove down the driveway, my brothers, Tyler and Coty, and I watched my dad jump off the hood of the car. My mom wasn't backing down. *What was so important about this place?* I wondered. *What did Cecil know that we didn't?*

I called my mom last night to give her a heads-up that I would be sharing this story with you. I was nervous because it's personal.

"He landed in a ditch," she said. "But he was fine, jumped right back up. You left out the time he pulled my spark plugs."

We both laughed hysterically. That is one of the other side effects to abnormality: laughter. People are sharing stories over dinner. You pause and share one from your childhood that you still get a kick out of. Everyone's face goes still. The room falls silent.

"I am so sorry," they mutter.

But you weren't looking for apologies. You thought you were just bonding. There can be healing in a chuckle. I think a lot of people who survive abnormal experiences such as this can look back and joke about it. How else do you make sense of crazy? There is power in our laughter.

Though the church building was new to me, the feeling of it wasn't. It was the same feeling I had when my mother came into my room to calm me down after another night terror. It was the same feeling I had when we would go to my aunt Michelle's house for the weekend to escape all the fighting. It was the same feeling I had sitting on my dad's mom's porch. I loved my granny and she loved us. Those places were peace for me. And church was peace for my mom.

Stained Glass Windows

I thought about all this when I pastored. How you never know what another person went through to even show up at church. You have no idea how difficult it may have been for them to get there. We should be incredibly welcoming when strangers step through our doors. Our faces may give them the first smiles they've seen in a long time. The greeters may be the most important part of your church service. You have no clue who is missing a spark plug. Everyone has something on the hood of their car.

Nothing significant happened in the service that day that Cecil rolled off the hood. I couldn't tell you what the sermon was. All I remember was how hard it had been to get there and how happy my mother was to be there. That was the day she traded late-night cries for late-night prayers. She traded today's pain for tomorrow's hope. She gave up broken promises for a promise of restoration. She left tainted words and found stained glass.

The phrase "I'll see you tomorrow" doesn't mean your relationships in life will all be perfect. In fact, you may be trapped in unbearable pain. The pain of a divorce. The pain of a betrayal. The pain of abandonment. The pain of broken trust. The pain of our own choices. The pain of a world that hasn't moved past racism. The pain of isolation. But on the other side of that legitimate pain is a knowing laughter. On that day my mother taught me one of the most important lessons I ever could have learned about faith: waiting for the ideal shouldn't prevent you from looking for what's possible. This is what it means to say, "I'll see you tomorrow."

What if, as human beings, we are stuck on a set of ideals that can't happen in a sinful world? That because we have been hurt today, it must rob us of our hope tomorrow? Jesus said, "With man this is impossible, but with God all things are possible" (Matt. 19:26). If human suffering was never God's original plan for the human race, life here on earth at this present moment isn't God's ideal plan for his creation either. Eden was ideal; earth is what became possible. What if you are so stuck on what wasn't ideal that you miss what is still possible?

My mother did what was possible, but it wasn't ideal. And growing up without a father present wasn't ideal for my brothers and me, but it was possible. Her choice to leave wasn't financially ideal either, so she picked up a few extra jobs and relied on family members to make it possible. Even as I write, I realize how much time I have wasted focusing on what wasn't ideal without searching for what was possible. Just as Heather had to learn to look for patterns and not isolated experiences, I had to stop focusing on the isolated incidents in my life. They may shape me, but they don't define me. For people who have experienced deep traumas, they can become stuck in trauma for decades after a troublesome event occurs—like a movie that just keeps playing over and over again. The deep pain caused by the trauma of betrayal, abuse, or abandonment was never God's ideal plan. But what if, with intensive counseling and new positive relationships and the redemptive work of the Holy Spirit, joy can still be possible? What if those one or two negative relationships from your past have kept you from forming ten others throughout the years that could've been positive? What if your disappointment today doesn't have to be the catalyst for tomorrow?

Stained glass changed the trajectory of our lives. What is so beautiful about stained glass is that during the medieval period it was more than a collage of beautiful colors in the walls of cathedrals. All the broken shards that were fused together told a story. Since 85 percent of the population couldn't read at that time, the stained glass portraits served as teaching pieces of art.[5] They captured scenes from Scripture that the clergy could use as an illustration to strengthen the people's faith. Stained glass windows not only told stories but directed the natural light to where it was needed. Stained glass portraits take time. They don't happen overnight. It takes time for an artist to create something from all the shards on his table. Every piece must pass through the artist's hand before it's placed with the others. What if our lives aren't all that different? What if God can make something beautiful out of all our broken pieces?

It Came to Pass

Scripture often uses the phrase "it came to pass."[6] This phrase, for example, regularly appears throughout the biblical story of Joseph (Gen. 37–50). What happens when what we hoped for tomorrow isn't just a day away? For Joseph, it was years, and yet it still came to pass. "It came to pass" represents something more than a single moment in someone's life. One commentary explained, "It hints not only that [events] happen, but that they are so soon over; they come, but they 'come to pass.' We do not always realize that, but it is always true. We are not conscious that the earth is moving round the sun, or that it is revolving daily on its axis, yet it is true. Summer and winter, day and night, do not cease, there is perpetual movement."[7]

One of the final times in the story of Joseph that we see the phrase "it came to pass" is in the last chapter of Genesis: "But as for you, ye thought evil against me; but God meant it unto good, to bring to pass, as it is this day, to save much people alive" (50:20 KJV).

The story of Joseph is one that understands "this, too, shall pass." It is one where he needed to press his sharp edges more firmly into God's hand instead of hiding them from him. If you're in a season where you are sitting in the pain of your promise, know that this, too, shall pass. Know that God is in the business of working with what is possible, not with what's ideal.

Shortly after that visit to church, my mother made the

decision to leave Cecil. To leave all of it. All the screaming, all the verbal and physical abuse, all the unpredictable behavior. She packed all of it up and stuffed it in her suitcase, and for years, wherever she went, I am sure she carried it with her. But you would never know it. That's the thing about meeting people: you have no idea what they've been through before they crossed your path. It wasn't too late for my mother, and it isn't too late for you. One woman changed the lives of her three sons and made a different tomorrow possible for them. We only get to tomorrow by living in today. We do what is possible, even if it's not ideal. Just as Scripture reminds us, "this, too, shall pass."

It Wasn't Ideal

Eighty percent of single parents are mothers.[8] The number of single mothers has risen over the years as divorce continues to climb at alarming rates. Dads disappear. Moms are left to carry it all. They must go to work, take care of the house, and raise the children. Meanwhile, the kids are left to watch. Little boys are raised to be tough and unbroken. That's what we've heard all our lives. Men train little boys to do manly things. They build campfires and pitch tents. They go fishing and teach you how to bait your own hook. Men patch holes and paint walls. But in my house, my dad was called Mom.

After my mother's season with Cecil came to pass, life didn't slow down. Growing up as the middle of three brothers, life was exciting. We weren't wealthy, so we never went to Disneyland or had extravagant family vacations. It was just my mother and her three boys. Looking back, my mom faced a greater struggle than we did. We had no dad to give us "the talk" or to teach us how to drive a stick, which meant my mom wore many hats, whether she wanted to or not. I learned to be a man from my mom.

My understanding of manhood came in the cards my mother dealt me. I know how to be a dad because of my mom. I make my wife's coffee first, because growing up I had a mom who ate last. I raise my daughter to be strong, because no one ever showed me that girls are weak. My son holds the door while people pile into the car. He's copying me. I copied Mom. Life is filled with jobs I don't want to do. Challenges that are easier to ignore than face. I face them anyway. People think that men are brave and don't back down, but it was a woman who taught me that. My mom is a fighter. She taught me to be a fighter too.

She showed me that God can make beauty from ashes and mountains from dust. Faith for me wasn't a man in a pulpit; it was a woman getting three kids dressed and using her last five dollars for gas. We got to where we were going on half petrol and half prayers. People argue over a woman's place in church, which I think is odd considering how many women have single-handedly brought entire families to heaven. Ask one in three kids in America who their shepherds are. My mom was my first pastor, and God ordained her. The world certainly needs more dads, but many of us have been sustained by moms.

I don't want to paint the picture that life suddenly became easier when we found God. My life has been anything but easy. For my entire adolescence I was depressed from my father's absence and then my brother's cancer. I would lose another seven years of my life before I started to feel like myself again. By my early twenties I found myself living in a trailer in Chattanooga, Tennessee, with no heat, inebriated almost daily, and wondering if I would ever feel whole again. My pain tormented me and prevented me from seeing a future for myself. My pain had me questioning if I would ever finish college or if I had the tools to be a dad. My pain numbed me to the point where I would cry out, *God help me. I just want to feel something again. I want to feel you again.*

It was at this time that all of my feelings started to compile, and my body reached a point that it could no longer function. I quickly learned that whatever emotions I held in would eventually manifest themselves physically if not properly dealt with. Just as Jose Rojas said to Heather, "Stress often has no warnings. It will just sit in your system patiently until your body breaks beneath it."

The combination of a poor lifestyle and deep grief caused me to start experiencing symptoms of post-traumatic stress disorder (PTSD). I woke up one morning and experienced the symptoms of vertigo. Everything was swirling and shifting around me and my balance was unsteady. My body was telling me that it had put up with enough. This wasn't something another beer was going to fix. I was twenty-one years old, and the last thing I wanted to do was talk about my feelings with some stranger who was getting paid to listen to me.

My life was put on hold and I was rushed to Michigan, where I visited every doctor you can imagine to help me figure out what was happening. I had brain scans and spinal taps. I was put on antidepressants and lost the ability to drive. Finally, I was put on six medications by one doctor in an attempt to correct my symptoms. I even went to the University of Michigan's hospital. For the most part, none of it helped. The root of my problem wasn't physical, though my issues were manifesting physically.

My problem was psychological. My brain couldn't carry my body any longer, pretending that I was okay. I wasn't okay.

By the way, during this time, nothing made me angrier than when someone would say my physical issues were a manifestation of my mental issues. I couldn't drive. I couldn't hold a job. I couldn't continue my education. I was constantly dizzy. I couldn't work out. This did not feel mental, and it infuriated me to hear that as a diagnosis. And yet the same summer I was at the end of my rope is the same summer I reconnected with Heather.

Slowly, I started to feel better. Sitting on Michigan piers with her made me feel less dizzy. Over the course of that summer, which turned into the fall, I weaned myself off of every antidepressant, anxiety, and sleeping medication I had been put on. For the first time in five years I started to feel like a person again. My relationship with Heather helped me to live again. I am not someone who will say all of us can get off prescription meds and just go to a small group. There are mental health conditions that we need medication to handle. As a former pastor, I am telling you, prayer plus prescriptions may bring you divine intervention. But I am also saying that relationship was part of my health journey that a doctor couldn't have prescribed for me.

I still struggle with seasonal depression. I probably always will. But opening myself back up to human beings after years of closing myself off has given me my life back.

I want to say this before you read the rest of my story. Relationships have been the greatest pain of my life, but they have also answered my deepest prayers. My PTSD and dysfunction and grief and self-hatred did not stem just from Cecil. Unfortunately, those pieces are much easier to talk about than the story I am about to share. The greatest trauma of my adolescence was not my parents' divorce or my absent dad. My grief digs much deeper. My wounds run much further. There are spaces in my life I can't even laugh about.

Till Tomorrow: Tyler

My adolescence was plagued by my brother's cancer. During his junior year of high school, Tyler had to face another round of chemotherapy. He was going to have to endure another season of his life being put on hold to face his worst nightmare, our worst nightmare. It was during a surgery that a doctor accidentally hit an important nerve in his back with a surgical instrument. This error caused Tyler to be paralyzed from the waist down. Not only was Tyler going to need several more rounds of chemotherapy, he was going to have to do it from a wheelchair. No more job at the mall. No more parties. No more basketball.

Tyler was fed up and begged us for a handgun. He wanted to end his life. He was in so much pain, paralyzed, and bloated from all of his treatments that he reached the point where he didn't want to live anymore.

One day I was helping him get dressed in the bathroom and he burst into tears.

"Look at me!" he cried. "I'm so ugly. My face looks like a balloon. I just want to die."

He had lost everything, and yet, somehow, Tyler went on to learn what it meant to live with what was possible. Without hope, he had nothing.

Maybe you feel the same way. I'll let you in on a secret: sometimes God gives us more than we can handle. Sometimes the ideal gets totally obliterated. And so we look to do what is possible.

Heather thinks that self-reliance is a myth. I agree with her. There have been so many moments and experiences my body couldn't handle. I needed my mother. I needed my brother. I needed my friends. There are times in my life when I should have reached out for support, but my instincts, as an introvert and untrusting of others, kept me suffering in silence.

Solitude isn't a bad thing; in fact, we all need moments of solitude to process and recenter ourselves spiritually, mentally, and emotionally. But *moments* of solitude are much different from living a *life* of solitude. Don't confuse solitude with isolation. I used to use the two words synonymously. I would say, "I like my alone time," but really I was just lonely. We need support. We need hope. We need prayer. We need people.

Tyler's story doesn't end with some miraculous healing, but it does end with what was possible. I wish I could tell you the day it happened, but I can't. I just remember a slow shift in Tyler's focus, even though he was in so much pain, still wondering what tomorrow would bring. This wasn't an instantaneous, sudden revelation. This was a gradual heart transformation. But I knew that prayer was at the center of it. He started to find purpose again, even though he was still surrounded by so much darkness. His chemo treatments proved successful, and he was adapting to life in a wheelchair. He was googling how much it would cost to have handicap equipment installed in his car so he could learn to drive with just his hands. He even said that he wanted to become a physical therapist so he could help people just like him.

And then, at one of his checkups, the doctor noticed the

tumor had come back. This time the cancer was all over his body. His spine, his bones, everywhere. It was a terminal diagnosis that gave him just a few short months to live. He was eighteen years old. The silence in the doctor's office that day was deafening. Total and complete silence. Our family buckled in pain. There was unspeakable brokenness. Our hope in restoration was shattered, and it didn't matter where we stepped, because every inch would cut us somewhere.

Prayer didn't bring healing. Our songs didn't bring strength. The anointing oil didn't bring any miracles. Over the next few months my brother's diagnosis proved true and his condition worsened. His body started to shut down as the cancer killed him from the inside out. Tyler was dying. We were too. Watching a teenager die is a process that steals every ideal. My life would never be the same. My mother's would never be the same. My little brother, Coty, would never be the same.

Even though Tyler's body was weakening, he decided he would still look for what was possible. Looking beyond this life, he turned to the possibility of what believing in the resurrection meant for him. During a time when he should've turned back to his feelings of anger and resentment toward God, he turned to the possibility of being with family someday in heaven. He looked beyond today and hoped for tomorrow.

During the final moments of his life here on earth, I remember sitting by his bedside as he slipped into a coma.

The hospice nurse said, "It won't be long now before he passes away."

I had never experienced such a deep loss like this before. And I had zero coping skills available to me to handle it. It shook me to the core of my very being. Just before Tyler took his last breath, he suddenly came to consciousness one last time. We were all amazed at what was happening.

He pulled me to his side and whispered in my ear, "Seth, at all costs you have to be there."

He went on to explain that even though he was dying, he was okay because he had found another possibility. He had found a different kind of hope. He had found a hope that says, no matter what happens today, *I'll see you tomorrow.*

He asked for the telephone, and one by one he started calling everyone he could think of in that moment. He called his cousin, his friends, his physical therapist. He even called our dad. Everyone. He told all of them that they had to be there too. That he had found a hope that was greater than pain. I know this may sound hard to believe as I tell it to you now, but all you would've seen is belief if Tyler would've told it to you then.

It wasn't long before Tyler slipped back into a coma. Moments before his passing, another supernatural incident took place. He started to shake his head violently, as if he were warring against something inside of him, something that was trying to steal his peace. And that's when it happened, a moment that our family will never forget. I am not exaggerating with the next words that came out of Tyler's mouth.

While shaking his head, he said, "Satan, get out of this room! Jesus is my King!"

As we all crowded around his bedside, it happened again.

Tyler started to shake his head back and forth. "Satan, get out of this room! Jesus is my King!"

And then, on November 18, 2004, just two days after his nineteenth birthday, my brother Tyler passed away. I am not trying to be a spiritual fanatic by telling you this story. I am telling you this story because it happened.

I am telling you this story because it opened my eyes that, until your last breath on this planet, the devil is trying to steal what's possible.

I am telling you this story because it testifies to the power of the gospel. That a nineteen-year-old boy on his deathbed can still find a "possible" amid life's greatest fear: death.

I am telling you this story because not all of your earthly relationships can find healing. Some will survive, but some will die.

I am telling you this story because it happened. And it taught me that bad things happen. And one day, if you'll let it, hope can still sit beside all of it.

This world will never give you what's ideal, but it also can't kill what's possible. I now have no doubt in my mind that heaven is a real place. Tyler was paralyzed and dying when he decided to dedicate his life to what's possible. We were baptized together a few months before he died. It was quite moving—his eighteen-year-old body being carried into the baptismal tank. And I've carried his faith with me ever since. His commitment created my possible. Scripture doesn't say that with God all things are ideal. It says that with God all things are still *possible*.

I see the world differently, not because of how Tyler died but because of how he lived. The decisions he made then changed the course of my life now. And I'm grateful to have been his brother. I truly believe people will be in heaven because of Tyler. Maybe the only reason I will be in heaven is because of Tyler.

What the devil means for evil, God can use for good. "We are hard pressed on every side, but not crushed; perplexed, but not in despair; persecuted, but not abandoned; struck down, but not destroyed" (2 Cor. 4:8–9). Joy is still possible.

I'll see you tomorrow.

• • • •

May the God who gives endurance and encouragement give you the same attitude of mind toward each other that Christ Jesus had. (Rom. 15:5)

ENGAGE

- *Who has kept you from growing?*
- *Think about something in your life that isn't ideal. What is still possible?*
- *What does it mean, practically in your life, to be hard-pressed but not crushed?*

CHAPTER 3

Running with the Tarahumara

*Running twenty-six miles is a feat that truly stretches
a human being. At the twenty-mile mark, someone
has said, the race is half over. Almost anyone can run
twenty miles, but the last six are the equivalent of
twenty more. Here the runner finds himself pushed to
the absolute limit. And therefore needs to call on those
hidden reserves, to use all the fidelity and courage
and endurance he has.*

GEORGE SHEEHAN

"What if you'll get to where you are going quicker by slowing
down?" my mentor asked.

I (Heather) am an achiever. For years my self-worth came
not from who I was but what I could produce. If I was pushing,

I had purpose. I didn't believe that God could love me if I didn't prove to him that I was lovable. I was a sprinter in college. It's honestly a metaphor for my entire genetic makeup. But what if life isn't meant to be sprinted? What if it's meant to be lived?

The second my mentor asked the question, a wave washed over me that felt like release. *What if you'll get to where you are going quicker by slowing down?*

He told me about the Tarahumara, a people from the Copper Canyon region of Mexico.[1] The Tarahumara are believed to be the best runners in the world. Kenyans may be faster at short distances, but there are few runners who could ever go the distance with the Tarahumara. People who have seen the Tarahumara in action say that, after twenty miles, they haven't even broken a sweat. An article on the subject said,

> In 1971, physiologist Dale Groom ran cardiovascular tests on Tarahumara adults and children, and concluded (as he'd write in the American Heart Journal), "Probably not since the days of the ancient Spartans has a people achieved such a high state of physical conditioning." Groom checked the pulse and blood pressure of Tarahumara runners during a five-hour race, and found their blood pressure went down while running, and their average heart rate—in the midst of banging out eight-minute miles—was only 130 beats per minute.[2]

Today, the Tarahumara are one of the most isolated people on the planet. Estimates are that only about forty thousand of them remain, and they still run races anywhere from one hundred to two hundred miles in the Copper Canyons, wearing nothing but sandals.[3]

"You aren't training for a sprint," my mentor said. "This is a two-hundred-mile run in the heat of Copper Canyon, with nothing but a pair of sandals. You can't rush through what makes you uncomfortable. No, we learn to run the race of life one step at a time."

The Tarahumara aren't "pushing through"; they don't even break a sweat. You aren't training for a sprint. With the reality of where everyone is in their mental, relational, and physical health today, this is a two-hundred-mile run in the heat of Copper Canyon in nothing but a pair of sandals. And what if we will get to where we are going faster if we all take a moment to slow down? Some doors can't be pushed open. Sometimes you need to walk, change the locks, buy new hinges, and sit with your back against the frame. You aren't alone while you are knocking. God has his hand over your fist. You may not be able to white-knuckle this. It takes a kid, on average, six months to grow a single inch. How long do you think it takes our minds to grow? Or our hearts? Or our character? Or our relationships? How do we face divorce with the lessons from the Tarahumara? How do we face grief, knowing this is not a sprint but a two-hundred-mile run? How do we balance work and hurt and pain and exhaustion with the pace of the Tarahumara? What if you will get to where you are going faster by slowing down?

We'll get where we're going, even if we're late

Slowing Down for People

I remember this very odd moment while I was living in Denver, where I felt incredibly alone. My friends, my closest friends, went to a party without me. We had been playing a board game with a couple we hung out with regularly on a Saturday night, and then I watched them pack up my little game pieces and leave. They were going to another couple's house to apparently have a game night party thing with several other people, none of which were us. I had thought we were *all* friends. In fact, I was the one who had even introduced them, but then I watched my game pieces get boxed up, and it literally felt like someone had turned off the neon sign and left Seth and me sitting in the dark while the crowd headed to the next location. (Seth and I actually bought our own neon sign that hangs over our coffee bar in our new house in Michigan. And we decide when it turns off.)

A group of our closest friends were all at a game night, and no one had thought to include us. Not even an obligatory, "Oh hey, did you all want to come?"

If you have ever heard that all your friends hung out in high school without you, you know exactly what I'm talking about, but strangely it feels worse in your thirties because we are all too old and tired for this. I can't worry about my credit score *and* being excluded from game night. As I watched them awkwardly leave, I looked at Seth and started crying.

"I don't think we have people who really love us here," I said. "Not like we did back home." (You already know I am dramatic.)

I called Scarlett and Vimbo and told them what had happened. They told me about similar experiences they had had. I was embarrassed to even say it out loud. A part of me is still embarrassed writing it now. That is the thing about slowing down. It's hard to find your pace when you're always sprinting to survive. When you are always having to save face or pretend you aren't hurt when you are. Do I say something, or do I let this go? Do I really want to be the thirtysomething woman asking for a sit-down meeting because no one invited me to Monopoly? I wanted my friends in Denver to somehow know in two years things about me that it took my friends back home decades to learn. I was judging them using a stick they couldn't possibly measure up to.

Adult friendships are hard—and awkward because a lot of our present conversations lack the context of our pasts. And we are all tired and insecure, and most of us have moved for jobs across the country, and we don't feel safe because even the people who know us don't really know us. It is so hard to slow down when the people who make life feel calm are in a different time zone.

I went on a walk with Tiffany down a trail called Waterton Canyon, and we watched mountain goats stand in the middle of our path, prompting us to go around them. There are so few straight paths. We laughed and we cried and not a single second felt awkward or forced. I remember having this moment where I realized that people did love me here, and I had to stop making snap judgments about my entire relationship with someone because of a single incident. Does one night of feeling left out cancel dozens of being brought in? You'll get to know people quicker when you are willing to slow down for them. And there is a lot of ground to cover. There is much we should be slowing down for.

Everything Has Changed

Many of us are overweight and emotionally eating. We are drinking to cope with our negative feelings and our grief. We are dealing with increased stress and anxiety, not to mention the financial devastation that has impacted so many people, and we are cutting off our friendships and families because we don't have time to invest in relationships. In a 1990 Gallup study, 26 percent of Americans said that when they go through a difficult time, a friend was the first person they would turn to. Today, according to a recent Gallup study, that has dropped by 10 percent, which means fewer Americans are relying on friends for emotional support, even though we are arguably going through increasingly difficult collective experiences. And it isn't like we are minimizing friendships so we can focus on family. Only 9 percent of Americans say that in a difficult time, they turn to a family member. So if we aren't turning to a friend and we aren't turning to family, who are we turning to? Ourselves, of course. According to the same study, 81 percent of Americans say that when making a big life decision, they rely on their own research.[4] That's right. For 81 percent of Americans, Google is our most trusted ally.

To be fair, 53 percent of people said they turn to their romantic partner, which is great for those of us in healthy marriages or relationships, but, still, there are some seven billion people in the world, and many of us will choose to consult only one of them when we face a difficult moment, if we choose to consult anyone other than Alexa at all.

We have to stop trying to white-knuckle our lives. We must stop trying to be our own best friends. We must stop trying to be our own therapists. Seth shared in the last chapter that God often gives us more than we can handle. Which is why we need each other.

One of my favorite verses is in Galatians: "Carry each other's burdens, and in this way you will fulfill the law of Christ" (6:2). What we cannot push through, together we can carry, and when we do this, we lift one another right toward Christ.

We must ask for help. Most of us aren't just suffering in silence; we are suffering in secret. Do you want to know what happened that day in Lakeside, Ohio, when I asked my mentor for help? It only strengthened our relationship. It became easier for me to ask for help later. It became easier for him to call and check up on me, just because. Asking for help doesn't hurt our relationships; it affirms them.

"You are not being attacked by the devil," my mentor told me calmly. "You are being attacked by yourself."

According to the American Psychological Association, 61 percent of adults said they experienced undesired weight changes since the pandemic.[5] When we were babies, if we wanted to be held or eat, we cried. It was our way of telling our caregivers that we needed something. A cry equaled human relationship or physical sustenance. And now, as adults, when we want to cry, we eat, because it is easier than turning to a friend or partner and saying, "I really need someone to hold me right now."

A 2021 *Harvard Health* article reported that eight out of ten Americans rate their stress level at an eight or more on a ten-point scale. When we are stressed our bodies release adrenaline, a hormone that, short term, tells us we don't need to eat, because we have a battle to fight. But if we stay in a constant state of stress, our bodies start to respond differently. They release cortisol, and cortisol (a stress hormone) increases our appetite.[6] We joke and say, "Oh, I am a stress eater," but for most of us, increased eating *is* a sign of stress.

I went through the McDonald's drive-through for the second time in a single day, and the lady at the window said, "Is that you again?"

"Shh, Brenda. Momma's stressed."

Studies show that our stress levels even change the types of food we crave. Some studies have shown that increases in our distress have a correlation with an increasing desire for high-fat, high-sugar foods. A 2021 *Harvard Health* article said that this is because high-fat, high-sugar foods help dampen the cortisol response in our emotions.[7] The idea of a "comfort food" is a legitimate medical condition. All employers should be forking over health insurance (pun intended). I have no footnote for that assertion; I just haven't been able to fit into my hot pants in a year and a half, and I think it's time for some compensation.

A 2020 Cleveland Clinic study examined how our appetites are affected by stress.[8] Participants were told to report stressful experiences that happened throughout their days—such as getting in a fight with your partner, an overwhelming deadline at work, and knowing there is some issue going on for your child at school. If this list were a bingo card, you would all owe me a lot of money. Participants who reported experiencing one stressor or more during a twenty-four-hour period burned 104 fewer calories after eating a high-fat meal than people who didn't report any stress. The researchers concluded that just one stressful event a day slows our metabolism so much that we could potentially experience a weight gain of eleven pounds over the course of a year. We aren't fat; we are stressed.

Nearly one in four adults have reported drinking more alcohol since the pandemic started.[9] Many of us went long periods without being with family or friends. Or maybe there was some uncertainty at work. Or "shelter in place" with your spouse was not the paradise your marriage was needing. So you bought a bottle of wine, told the kids it's time to go to sleep for the twentieth time, and turned on some *Downton Abbey* because you deserve it. That margarita was helping you cope with stress. It released endorphins and boosted serotonin levels. This short-term fix doesn't make you a monster, but it may cause you to avoid reality, which can lead to more serious issues down the road. This can lead someone who is new to alcohol coping mechanisms into accidental long-term dependence.[10] Most people who become alcoholics do so quite by accident. You don't have to deal with your emotions, you don't have to face your feelings, you don't have to admit you are drowning. Drinking may allow you to feel better, but with 23 percent of adults saying they are drinking more to cope since the pandemic, it is always important to look at our motivations for every unhealthy coping mechanism we reach for.

Another wave that has hit us since the pandemic is the tightening of our social circles. Friends we were happy to keep casual relationships with became draining to maintain. Something happened in the wake of a pandemic and social unrest that caused us to say, "I quit." In some cases, COVID-19 has given us the perfect excuse to finally cut off the relationships we were barely holding on to anyway.

In a 2021 Pew Research Center article, it was found that the number-one impact on American lives since COVID has been how it has affected our relationships.[11] People have lost touch with family and friends, and many adults describe deep feelings of isolation as a result of increased loneliness. And it isn't just Americans who are suffering. A study from the University College of London found that over a fifth of adults say they have experienced a total breakdown of a relationship with either friends, family, colleagues, or a romantic partner since COVID.[12] People have fewer friends than ever before, and they talk to the friends they have less than they did prepandemic. Americans have even reported relying on their friends less for emotional support.[13]

Forget Your Feelings

"Forget your feelings," my mentor said.

I had just gone on and on about how unfairly I was being treated.

"Heather." He paused from eating his fries and looked up at me gently. "If all it takes for you to quit is for someone to be willing to hurt your feelings, you will never make it."

His voice got firm now. "You think the devil can't find someone to hurt your feelings? Eventually, leaders have to lead."

My whole face went numb, not because I was upset, but because I knew he was right. I needed to acknowledge my feelings without being controlled by them. Feelings are important indicators, but when it comes to destructive feelings, we can't let them direct all our choices. Listen to love, listen to empathy, listen to sadness and cautiousness, but I would be very careful with letting destructive thoughts drive your car. Negative thoughts are an indicator that you need to assess a context. Bitterness is an indicator that you need to ask yourself what is making you feel disappointed or afraid. But I think letting

56

negative thoughts drive your car may lead you to a destructive destination. I had to learn to stop letting antagonistic people take up so much space in my head. I had to think bigger than any singular conflict.

"What is my long game?" is a question I ask myself a lot. "What would be the short-term impact of this choice or my sending this message or my saying these words? And how does that impact my long game?"

Seth will go deeper into this conversation in the next chapter, but asking myself this question while assessing a current conflict has been so helpful to my deciding what emotion I am going to let drive my car. I like to wallow. It is honestly part of my acceptance process. When something bad happens, I give myself a few days to binge *Survivor* episodes and let my house sit in squalor. And then I repeat to myself what Jose so delicately said to me: "The devil is always going to find someone willing to hurt your feelings. But at some point, leaders have to lead."

Of course, this mantra is not to be used unilaterally. Seth will walk you through situations that will require more than a couple of days and are beyond what *Survivor* can fix. But so much of our life is not big things. Our day-to-day is filled with dozens of little things. Dozens of pinpricks that, if we aren't careful, we can allow to take over our lives. Dozens of small steps that, if we aren't vigilant in how we take them, will trip us. Dozens of triggers. Stewing over people's ignorance isn't going to make them care, but it will deplete our energy.

My friend and TikTok sensation Kevin Spencer Wilson (@ crossculturechristian) said to me the other day when we were talking about trolling, "When I am on a run, and I see dog poo on the street, am I going to stop and stare at it? Am I going to analyze it and wonder why it is there and who left it? Am I going to let it stop my run?"

I have repeated Jose's words to myself over the years. How hard do you think Satan has to look to find someone willing to hurt your feelings? For most of us, it doesn't take a Google search. He can probably find someone in our own family or workplace or church. He doesn't even have to scroll through our social media. Feelings are important, and they are often crucial indicators of something internal, but they can't be the lord over our lives. So many of my decisions for years were based on my feelings. One time I was upset about how my work was treating me, so I quit. I made a rash decision and spent the next year scraping by to make ends meet. Logically I should have waited until I had another job before I quit my current one. But I didn't feel like waiting. I felt like sticking it to them by quitting. Next thing I knew I was eating rice and beans for weeks, and I don't think my former employer was taking it as hard as I was. They scrambled for about seven days to replace me, but the income I lost bled my bank account for months. Our feelings cannot determine all of our choices.

Do you think Martin Luther King Jr. faced dogs and fire-hoses because he felt like it? No. He did it because leaders lead. Did Mother Teresa always *feel* like surrounding herself with excruciating poverty and starvation? Did Michael Jordan put in all those early gym mornings because it felt good? (No one feels good on mile twenty-six!) Some of our greatest inspirations, athletes, and thought leaders did what they had to even when they didn't want to. Because often the path to greatness is on the other side of some uncomfortable hurdle you thought you'd never break through.

You must do the work without the worship. You must believe in the cause more than the cost. I wanted my mentor to coddle me, to tell me that bad people were bad and good people deserved better. But he didn't. He told me I didn't have time to think like that. Life isn't fair, and the higher the level, the higher the devil. What if you were meant to lead?

My friend Annie F. Downs said to me, "Heather, it's okay to be sad. It's okay to be discouraged. Feelings aren't bad. You can tell them to get in the car. They can even pick the music. But faith drives."

That's what I want for you. Tell your feelings they aren't bad. Tell them they can get in the car, ride shotgun, and even pick the music. But faith drives.

Learning to Pace Yourself

The Leadville Trail 100 is an ultramarathon held annually in Colorado. It started in 1983 and is a one-hundred-mile race where fewer than half of the people who start it finish it in the thirty hours allowed. Want to know how we even know about the Tarahumara? Because in 1993 a few of their racers showed up at the starting line. Christopher McDougall, author of *Born to Run*, observed,

> Breaking the tape, in a time of 20:03:33, was 55-year-old Victoriano Churro, a farmer and the oldest of the three Tarahumara. He was followed by Cerrildo Chacarito in

second and Manuel Luna in fifth. The three Tarahumara were still bouncing along on their toes as they crossed the line.

Their performance proved to be no fluke. A year later, another Tarahumara runner, Juan Herrera, would win at Leadville, finishing in 17:30:42 and chopping 25 minutes off the course record. Then in 1995, three Tarahumara finished in the top-10 of the rugged Western States 100 in California.[14]

The Tarahumara, in their shorts and sandals, beat people who had trained for this race their entire professional careers. And it isn't that they have trained themselves to run so hard that they ignore that their bodies are pleading to stop, and it isn't that they are walking so slowly they didn't show up to compete. The Tarahumara have somehow managed to do what I think my mentor wanted me to learn if I was going to start showing up to my life as if it mattered: they had learned how to run their race at a pace they could maintain. The goal is to leave everything we have on the track in a way that fills us to keep going rather than depletes us so we can barely finish. I think this is what the prophet Isaiah meant when he wrote, "Those who hope in the LORD will renew their strength" (40:31). I think it perfectly describes the Tarahumara, a people who learned how to "run and not grow weary," how to "walk and not be faint." Striking that balance between our work and our rest is what will produce higher-quality work. Remember what my mentor asked me: "What if you'll get to where you are going quicker by slowing down?"

It's similar to growth. If a child wants to grow, she must sleep. Our bodies produce growth hormones while we sleep. If a nine-year-old wants to grow taller over the summer, he will get there faster by slowing down. What if the race God is training you for would be impossible to sprint? What if God is looking for people like the Tarahumara? People who know how to breathe and when to breathe so they can sustain the journey, even if all the world ever gives them is a pair of ragged sandals.

When Seth said earlier, "Waiting for the ideal shouldn't prevent you from looking for what's possible," I had goose bumps. I literally slapped his arm when I read it and said, "Babe, this is brilliant!" It is truly how I want to live my life: one step at a time. One possible to the next. If you can't run right now, walk. If you can't push any longer, slow down. If you can't keep looking at the same situation, rest your eyes. If you can no longer swim, float. Turn the car off. Stop for gas. The reality is that we have all, collectively, been through a lot. So as you come heading toward another lap, look for the people who are cheering you on. Take a moment to soak in the voices who are yelling your name. Life is not just about finding God; it is about surrendering to the God who found you.

What if you'll get there faster by slowing down? More important than winning or losing is finding a pace you can sustain. May we take nothing in this life for granted. May we run the race set before us, like the Tarahumara. May we renew our strength. We grow while we rest.

Maybe you didn't know it, but you'll be taller in the morning.

• • • •

If you have raced with men on foot and they have worn you out, how can you compete with horses? (Jer. 12:5)

ENGAGE

- *Discuss the verse from Jeremiah 12. What does that mean?*
- *What does it mean, "You'll get there faster by slowing down"?*
- *Are there any coping skills you have picked up recently that you think may not be good for you?*

CHAPTER 4

The Infinite Game

We were defined by what we did. What we had to do.
I think this is why guys like football, and why they
join the army, because as long as you are playing the
game or following orders you do not have to figure out
who you really are.

PETE HAUTMAN

"I am not sure I believe in God anymore."

Those were the words of Kyle, a young EMT, who sat across the table from me (Seth) in a pancake restaurant. I sat in silence, waiting for him to explain his reason for letting go of something that had been such a big part of his life for so many years when he was growing up.

We had just met. This was our first meal together, and I was new to pastoring. I found out that Kyle had attended a private school, grew up in a youth group, and had Christian parents who prayed for him, and yet he wanted nothing to do with God. I know a lot of people like Kyle.

He went on to explain that his faith was strong until the past year, when he started working as an EMT. Kyle said, "When you've seen the pain that I have, you find it hard to understand where God is in all of it."

I know a lot about pain. I know a lot about "where is God" questions. I have asked them. I said a silent prayer for wisdom and nodded for Kyle to go on. This breakfast wasn't about what I knew; it was about listening to Kyle.

He explained how he recently had pulled a dead baby from a car that had been hit by a drunk driver.

"The drunk driver was fine. The baby wasn't," he said.

The images were burned into his mind. I know what it feels like to try and unsee something. I wish it were as easy as simply closing your eyes. For some of us, that's where the pain is.

"If you could've seen the mother, you would understand what I'm talking about. Her baby had just been taken from her without notice. Tell me, where is a loving God in all that pain?"

Part of listening to people is knowing when they are really asking you a question or when they are asking you to listen. Kyle wasn't looking for a sermon. He was looking for an answer to pain. I knew the Christian colloquialisms; I knew the scriptures and the bullet points. I knew I could talk about sin and choices. I knew I could tell him my own "where is God" story. But part of pastoring and part of walking with Christ is knowing when to rely on what you know and when to ask God for help. *Help* is the prayer of every Christian traveler. Don't be afraid to say it. I knew about pain, but I didn't know Kyle. I couldn't possibly know what he needed to hear from me, but I knew someone who did.

I closed my eyes for a minute and asked God for the words. I didn't need to defend God; I needed to invite him. This was my first big crisis of faith as a new pastor, and I was in over my head. I knew that whatever I said could be make-or-break for Kyle. I may just be the last pastor he ever tried to talk to. My words would hold eternal weight.

Lord, I prayed, *Kyle is in pain. Please show up and give me the words to speak. He's your child. Show him you are here. Show him it is okay to ask hard questions.*

I opened my mouth and started to say something, still unsure of where I was going at first but trusting that God had a plan. I took a long, deep breath between every word.

"Kyle, God was there at the accident, because God was in you."

His eyes opened wide.

I continued, "God was present that day because you caringly pulled the baby from the car. He was present through your comforting actions toward that grieving mother. He was there as you held her while she cried. God is in you."

If you have never experienced the hands of God through the hands of another person, this may fall flat for you. But when my brother died, I saw God in my mom. When I was diagnosed with PTSD, I saw God in my wife. When I moved out to Tennessee, I saw God in my friend Zack who dropped everything to go with me. Things you think you will never live through, you find yourself living through, and usually it is only because someone else walked through it with you. It doesn't fall flat when you've known what it feels like to be seen by another person. And it changes the way I engage with the world when I remember that God wants to live in me. God is in you. And if people can't see God, it is because we are no longer image bearers.

My encounter with Kyle taught me so much about what it means to be present in a world of suffering. It doesn't mean that everything is going to be ideal. Human suffering is far from ideal. But for believers, we are to walk by faith, not by sight. Whether in season, or out of season, we walk even if we don't feel it. We walk even if we don't know where we are walking to. Like the Tarahumara, we find a pace that we can maintain and we go for the distance, not a sprint. We walk even though we can't see it. In a sermon, Steven Furtick said, "The miracle is not in our feelings, it is in our feet."[1] You kept walking, and that's the miracle.

Finite vs. Infinite

Bestselling author and speaker Simon Sinek observed that in game theory, a theory known to social scientists and economists, there are infinite games and finite games.[2] A finite game is a single basketball game or even a season. It comes and goes, and it's easy to distinguish the winners from the losers, because there are a fixed set of rules and players that dictate how the game is played. An infinite game, according to Sinek, is something like the game of business. He explained the players may be Apple or Microsoft or Amazon, but over time the players will change out. The goal is simply to perpetuate the game.[3]

The game of basketball was developed in 1891 by James Naismith.[4] He was thirty-one and working for the YMCA. He was trying to develop a sport that would allow athletes to stay in shape while also staying warm in the wintertime. He asked a janitor if he could have two square boxes. He ended up nailing two peach baskets to the rail of the gymnasium balcony. It just happened to be a ten-foot rail. The first game ever played turned into a blood fest. People hit and kicked. Boys tackled one another as if they were playing football. Players received black eyes. You would not have known this was the beginning of a multibillion-dollar industry. By 1905 high schools had picked up the game that started with two peach baskets as an official winter sport.

A single game of basketball could be considered finite because it has a fixed set of players in each game, and once it's played, it's over. On the other hand, the *sport* of basketball itself is potentially infinite. It has been around since 1891. There is game after game and season after season. The players simply get swapped for new ones, and the sport continues to be played. In one season a particular team may be at the top of its success, and a decade later it can be the worst team in the NBA. This is what Michael Jordan understood about the game of basketball when he was cut from his high school team. He understood that a finite game, or even a finite season, with a fixed set of rules, couldn't impact the infinite rules of the sport.

Jordan had more than resilience; he had a mindset that could see beyond a single score or a single season. He saw beyond the finite and knew the infinite sport would come back every October and could be played again until June—if you made the playoffs. And with that new season came new opportunities for another winner to emerge. As Jordan's career continued, he began to understand if he wanted there to be another season of victory, he needed a team. He said, "Talent wins games, but teamwork and intelligence wins championships."[5]

What if our lives aren't all that different from basketball? What if we have fixed seasons too? Just like with Kyle, certain seasons will cause us to question if God was ever with us at all. But what if God was never meant to be seen in a single season? What if God is meant to be seen in you? For example, a job loss, the sudden death of a loved one, or a betrayal of friendship? What if we understood that we're not players in a finite game but players in an infinite one? That there is a new season approaching, and our ability to finish strong depends on the kind of team we are building right now. What if, like Jordan, it's the mindset we cultivate in the off-season that makes the difference the next October? Two peach baskets turned into a multibillion-dollar industry. You may be surprised at what can happen when you start to play the game.

When we grasp that life on earth isn't a solo sport and we learn to play with our team, we go further. Our team consists of marriage, friendships, and families. What if we've got it all wrong, and our goal isn't to win a single game but to cultivate the stamina to simply keep playing the game with one another? What if winning doesn't look like scoring? What if it looks like assists? What if it looks like rebounds? What if it looks like knowing when to pass? What if playing looks like just showing up? We would need a team to do that. Consider your team to be the inner circle of people you interact with every day. Whether it's your spouse, your friends, your children, the people at your workplace, it's whoever you interact with on a daily basis.

The game of life isn't a solo sport. It's a team sport. The goal isn't to just keep playing. It's to keep playing *together*. You may be able to play a quarter by yourself, but we are called to play the long game. That's done through community. We win together and we lose together. We are called to see beyond today's disappointments with the people we live in community with and still see their value. If there's one thing this nation is desperate for after all the political carnage and isolation caused by COVID, it's community. It's remembering that humanity was always called to play the infinite game. The players may change, but the game of life continues.

So, what if the age of self-sufficiency is over and a new one has begun? A season where we recognize we need each other in order to keep on playing? One that learns to pass the ball and leans on our teammates to get the rebound ? One that understands it's okay to have a seat on the bench because there are other players in the game as well? There is a reason why Christ chose twelve disciples and not just one. He needed a team. He saw their potential and knew they would go further together in accomplishing his mission if the twelve learned to play as one.

Jesus said, "My prayer is not for them alone. I pray also for those who will believe in me through their message, that all of them may be *one*, Father, just as you are in me and I am in you. May they also be *in us* so that the world may believe that you have sent me" (John 17:20–21, emphasis added).

What if like when James Naismith created basketball, God has called you to build a team that will keep people warm even in the wintertime? The game of basketball had humble beginnings, but it grew as more people learned about the game. James thought he was creating a finite game, but he ended up lighting a match to an infinite sport. God's will is to be in you. When Jesus prayed, he prayed that we, together, as a people, would become a team. "That all of them may be one," he said. Faith is not a solo sport. You are meant to join an infinite team. Get your jersey. Lace up your shoes. Let's strike a match and start a blaze like this world has never seen.

One of the most beautiful aspects of basketball isn't the court but the bench. The bench is a reminder that, if you need a moment, there is a place where you can have a seat and collect yourself. The bench has people you can tag in when you take an elbow to the face. The bench is a sacred covenant between a player and the team. It says, "We are in this with you, and you won't win or lose this game alone." Heather ran track, but her best race was a relay. She didn't do it by herself; she competed with her team.

"I will," Jesus prayed, "that all of them may be one."

Our faith experience wasn't meant to be played out in isolation. Where is your bench? Where is your sacred space where you can ask, "Where is God in all of this?" Who are the people cheering you on while you play the game but also willing to get their own hands dirty if you need some assistance?

People Who Climb Sometimes Fall

I almost died. It happened just over a year ago. Hudson, my oldest son, and I were preparing for our annual father-son overnight backpacking trip that had become a tradition over the past few years. We stocked up on gummy bears and ramen noodles and headed for the mountains. We were excited to go and explore this territory together. I was sure this was going to be a time of much-needed rejuvenation for the both of us.

I woke up the next morning at 4:30 a.m. to peel Hudson off the bed where he'd been sleeping. I wanted to hit the trail by daybreak so we would have as much time as possible to set up camp and explore our new surroundings. About an hour into the trip Hudson started to feel tired and wanted to find a spot where we could set up our base camp. We were hiking the Ben Tyler Trail outside of Bailey, Colorado, and we were on a path that was perfectly etched into the mountain landscape. We searched for a while, but it was hard to find a level spot to set up camp. I remember seeing what I thought looked like a nice spot just off the trail. I quickly dropped my pack and raced up a few boulders in hopes of discovering a good campsite at the top of my trek. I was wrong. There were tree stumps everywhere, and that doesn't make for a good night's sleep.

That's when it happened. I placed my foot on what seemed to be a steady boulder, and on my way down the massive rock suddenly came loose. That boulder broke free from the mountain-side, and I went tumbling down with it. Everything became a blur as I hurtled down the side of the mountain for about twenty-five yards before rolling over a ten-foot drop-off. *Did this really just happen?*

My body from my waist down was completely numb from the impact. For a few seconds I lay there half-conscious in a mangled ball on the ground before I started to assess my wounds. That's when I realized I had been severely injured. When I went to feel my back, I couldn't feel a thing. My hand was covered in blood, and all I knew was I wasn't in good shape. That's when it hit me.

Hudson!

In a panic I wondered if he had been injured too. My

adrenaline kicked in and I started yelling his name as I clawed my way back to the trail. What if something had happened to him when I fell? That uncertainty hurt worse than my fall. When I found him, he was fine. In fact, he didn't realize what had just taken place. Somehow he hadn't seen me fall. It was as if God put blinders over his eyes and covered his ears for that moment in time.

I knew we weren't walking out of the mountains without help. I started yelling for someone to rescue me, and within minutes a shadowy figure appeared on the trail ahead of me. Was I hallucinating? I yelled louder until the figure in the distance took form. It was a guy in his midtwenties. He said his name was Ryan, and he had been on an early morning hike with his fiancée. Ryan told me he heard my voice in the distance. He was a trained wilderness first responder. An overwhelming feeling of relief rushed over my entire body. *Really, God?* The only person hiking the trail that morning besides Hudson and me was a wilderness first responder! I didn't take that as a coincidence.

After he assessed my wounds, Ryan told me I had been punctured on my backside and the wound looked very deep. He helped me walk out of the forest that day by carrying my backpack and half my body weight in his arms. He then drove us back home in my truck. After the two-hour trip, my wife quickly slipped into the driver's seat and rushed me to the emergency room.

I remember the fall. I saved the bloodstained pants. I remember that feeling of total helplessness. But more than that, I remember the fear and I remember Ryan. For some reason when I pray, I often look for something visible, like a burning bush—the one Moses found on Mount Sinai. I want a helicopter to appear from the heavens and the voice of God to boom from the clouds and say, *Seth, do not fear.* There are so many times in life when I am in my off-season, and I am looking for an incredible manifestation of God's presence to surround me in order for me to believe I am still worthy. But the Scripture has only one burning bush. There is only one Jericho. There is only one Red Sea incident. It is actually incredibly rare for a sea to drown an army. Those are the great stories that the people of Israel were told to remember to carry them through the hundreds and thousands of years in between. But do you want to know what probably happened daily? God showed up through Ryans. Even greater than *seeing* the people of faith who change the course of someone else's history is *becoming* them. Not seeing a Ryan in your life shouldn't stop you from being a Ryan in someone else's. People will ask, "Where is God?" But God is in you through the power of the Holy Spirit and the examples of how Jesus lived and loved here on earth.

Moving Backward

Healing from that mountain injury took two months, and eighteen months later my lower back still has a spot that is completely numb from the fall. There are pieces of us, after a fall, that may feel numb for a long, long time. But we are still here. We are still alive. The danger of climbing is always falling. But for any hiker, the greater fear is never climbing at all. Before the fall I was a reckless hiker going on twenty-plus-mile hikes in high elevations by myself without leaving a clear map of where I was going and word of what time rescue dogs should be sent out if I wasn't home. I took my safety for granted until that day when everything changed. Have you ever experienced a situation that changes the way you see and approach everything around you? An event happens that shakes you so badly, your brain fires off caution warnings even in moments when it isn't needed? Falling changes us.

I trusted the wilderness. It had always been a place of peace and safety until it showed me another side of itself. Now, every time I enter the mountains, I do so with a sense of fear, knowing that any decision to take another step forward could cost me everything. That is a classic trauma response. Our brain is alerting us when we walk into experiences that have hurt us before that we must be careful or we may fall again. And we can choose to let that fear keep us from climbing. We can stay on the ground. We can camp right there in safety. But is it possible that safety is an exceptionally high price to pay for living?

I knew if I wanted to enjoy the mountains again, I would need to eventually go back to the spot where my fall happened. Sometimes we must go in reverse if we want to move forward. And I became more careful. Heather made me buy a GPS. I email the route that I'll be hiking to at least two people. I no longer do solo twenty-plus-mile hikes. My pain has made me a more calculated hiker. I now understand there is a great risk associated with every adventure. But those risks are not worth forfeiting the adventure. I've seen some of the most beautiful sunrises. I have walked beside mountains that made me feel so small.

Phil Moore, one of my favorite theologians, wrote, "Pharaoh's rule was depicted by a cobra on his crown."[6] God turned Moses' staff into a cobra in the wilderness before he sent him to Egypt, and told him to "take it by the tail." God essentially was showing Moses that he would put even Pharaoh into his hand.

God sent Moses in reverse before he could move him forward. Before the sea was parted, before the miracle of the manna in the desert, before the Ten Commandments were written by the finger of God, there was a cobra that had to be grabbed by its tail. Moses had to confront the place that caused him so much pain for the past forty years. Moses had to confront Pharaoh. What do you need to confront before you can move forward?

Where divorce failed me and my brothers, God has asked me to grab that by the tail. I can do better for Heather and my three kids than my dad did for me. But I must confront the cobra. I must grab its tail. Situations where I failed in my past and let my anger get the best of me, God has called me back to those cobras too. Sometimes we reverse before we can move forward. Times when I have been stuck in my grief, God has called me to grab those cobras by the tail. I have sat beside the beds of dying people. I have been the one with the anointing oil. I can sit in rooms with people who are dying because I have been in a room where my whole world was dying and someone sat by me.

God wastes nothing. Not even our failures or trauma. What if he can use our pain to his glory? He often calls us back to those painful places so he can finish the story. Moses had a few bad falls, but God still took him to another mountain. You may be waiting for your burning bush. Maybe your "where is God" question is drowning out any other meaningful conversation. Life is an infinite game, even when we don't understand what is happening at the end of a single season. But here is what I know for sure: God was in Kyle and God was in Ryan and God would like to be in you.

The mountaintops are beautiful. And starting to climb today may allow you to see it tomorrow.

• • • •

He will command his angels concerning you to guard you in all your ways. (Ps. 91:11)

ENGAGE

- *What do you think safety may be costing you?*
- *Have you ever had a moment when you saw God in another person?*
- *Have you ever had someone tell you they saw God in you?*

CHAPTER 5

Start with No

"No" is a complete sentence.

ANNE LAMOTT

"Are you breaking up with me?" My (Heather) voice cracked. I was supposed to be getting married in two months. How do you make alternative plans for the end of your future? He was the only plan I had.

"I don't want to marry you anymore," he said coldly.

Did you know your ears never stop hearing? Even when you are sleeping, you are hearing. Your brain just stops paying attention to the sounds.[1] I was awake. My eardrums were vibrating according to each word, but my brain had stopped paying attention to the sounds his mouth made. I don't remember his reasoning. Everything went silent.

He broke up with me a lot. It was his form of punishment.

If I did something he didn't like, if I told the wrong person the wrong thing, if I ignored a phone call, he would punish me. The punishment was typically a withdrawal of affection.

"I'm not talking to you for a week."

"I'm not going to see you for three days."

"I am breaking up with you."

Today, he was calling off our wedding. How did I get here?

I was a smart girl. I had good parents and a great relationship with my dad. I was brought up in a conservative Christian home. But when I hung up the phone, I realized I wasn't proud of who I was anymore. My relationship looked nothing like what my parents would have wanted for me. In May 2009 I learned perhaps one of the most important lessons I would ever learn when it comes to relationships: they aren't all worth fighting for.

Knowing When to Leave

My ex-fiancé had a horrible temper. He was also extremely manipulative. He was very good at making me feel sorry for him, and so, even though I knew the patterns and behaviors we were serving each other weren't healthy, I didn't know how to stop it. To be honest, I didn't know if I wanted to stop it. He was what I knew, and in between the toxicity, there was love. He was crazy about me. In fact, that is why he was always so angry and jealous, because I was so special. He punished me because he loved me so much. At least, this is what he'd explain when we were back on again.

Licensed social worker Ari Hahn noted that while punishment is effective in a parent-child relationship, it is not effective for adult-adult relationships.[2] He observed that partnership should be the goal of adult-adult relationships. When we set up one partner with the ability to hand out reward and punishments, we create an imbalance in the power dynamic of our relationship. Healthy relationships, even healthy Christian relationships, are based on equality. I don't think we should apply this just to our romantic relationships. This is key for healthy friendship dynamics too. Healthy relationships make you healthier. If your relationships are making you sicker, it may be time to leave.

Hahn wrote, "More abusive forms of emotional punishment can include acts of revenge like, 'I'm not going with you to your parents because you didn't treat me right at dinner.'"[3] My ex used to do this sort of thing a lot. I did not want to be embarrassed by having to explain to my family why he suddenly did not join me for a gathering, so it was a surefire way for him to emotionally extort our relationship boundaries.

He never hit me, not with his fists, but certainly with his words. Your brain has a shared circuitry between physical pain and emotional pain.[4] This is why we use physical language to describe emotional destruction: "that was such a slap in the face," "you tore my heart out," "it feels as if you stabbed me in the back." We are using physical language to describe what happens emotionally because our brains process them the same way. The anterior insula and the anterior cingulate cortex (don't worry, I will not quiz you later) are lighting up whether someone punches you with words or with their fist.[5] "Words will never hurt me" is not true. Our brains receive the pain of words quite similarly to the pain of fists. And some of us are being beaten from the inside out.

One study took this concept a step further. They put people

who had experienced social rejection into two groups: one group was given a placebo and the other was given acetaminophen (Tylenol) for three weeks after a rejection incident.[6] People who received the Tylenol reported fewer hurt feelings than people who received the placebo. When the researchers did a brain scan to look at the anterior insula and the anterior cingulate cortex (areas of your brain that process physical pain, but, again, no quiz), they found there was less activation in this region for the people who took the Tylenol. Now no one is telling you to take an Advil to get over your grief—please see a therapist and talk through what options are available—but I do want to hammer home the point that physical and emotional pain are linked.

People can quite literally break our hearts. A slap to the face and a slap to the heart are processed in the same way in our brains. And so, just as no one should stay in a relationship that is physically abusive, you shouldn't stay in an emotionally abusive relationship either. You need a cast. You need medical attention. You need a heart and mind doctor. Imagine how crazy you would look after a car accident and breaking several bones if you then walked into work like nothing happened. And yet that is what so many of us are doing every single day. Showing up to work, with all these broken pieces. Showing up to class, trying to learn, with all these bleeding cuts. We are being treated badly by family, coworkers, or friends, and then we expect ourselves to still perform all of our other duties. What would you do if you were in a car accident today? You would lie down. You would see a doctor. You would certainly not shrug it off and say, "I'm fine." You must know when to leave. It is imperative to talk about the boundaries a person has crossed in your life with a therapist or with other close loved ones. I want to focus most of my perspective in this book on how we can stay. Not everyone is abusive, and not every pain a trauma. But as Seth will confirm, it would be irresponsible of either of us to tell you to stay if we don't first tell you that sometimes you need to leave.

No!

Every time before a plane takes off, the flight attendants warn you about what to do if the aircraft loses oxygen: "Should the cabin lose pressure, oxygen masks will drop from the overhead area." And then they say something that sounds cruel, but it may just save your life.

"Please place the mask over your own mouth and nose before assisting others."

Oxygen masks are deployed on a plane when the oxygen in the cabin is dangerously low. It gets so low, you may quickly lose consciousness by trying to help the person next to you. If that happens, everyone dies. So, instead, the advice given to us every time we fly is to place the mask over our own mouths before assisting others. In life, some of us are trying to pass out masks, and we are dying for lack of air.

I believe this point is also biblical. T. D. Jakes tells the story of the ten virgins in Matthew 25.[7] In this story, five virgins are wise and five virgins are foolish. The term *virgins* in Scripture often represents the church. The symbolism is that these women represent a pure faith. The only difference between the ten symbols of the church is that some are wise and some are foolish, but all of them have faith. The wise virgins have enough oil, and the foolish ones do not. In Scripture the symbolic meaning of oil refers to the Holy Spirit.

John McKinley, an associate professor of theology at Biola University, explained, "I am not saying that every reference to oil (200x) in the Bible is a symbol for the Holy Spirit's involvement, but I am saying that every reference to anointing implies either a plea for the Spirit's action (as in consecration or healing) or a revelation of the Spirit's presence to empower individuals (as for prophets, priests, and kings)."[8]

Jesus' parable reads, "Then all the virgins woke up and trimmed their lamps. The foolish ones said to the wise, 'Give us some of your oil; our lamps are going out'" (Matt. 25:7–8).

But in verse 9, I want you to see what T. D. Jakes reminded us is the first word that these wise virgins told the fools: "No."

I want you to read those two letters again: "No."

I want you to say it out loud, wherever you are: "No!"

Wise people know how to say no!

Wise people know it is imperative that they put the mask on themselves before trying to assist someone else. I think part of the problem in today's church culture is that all of us are running out of oxygen, we have very little oil in our lamps, but rather than making sure we experience the Holy Spirit for ourselves and have an intimate relationship with Jesus that is sustaining the reality of our own needs, we try to give to people what we don't even have.

Remember the Tarahumara in chapter 3.

Remember the infinite game Seth said we are playing in chapter 4.

What are you doing spiritually to ensure that you can continue to play in the infinite game? What are we doing relationally through healthy boundaries to make sure we can run two hundred miles through Copper Canyon?

The secret to a pace that can sustain the journey is an intentional filling of your oil. There is no greater relationship you will ever have than your relationship with God. His cup will never run dry. We can't hear from God regularly if we aren't taking time to listen to God regularly. How often do you do that? Rather than talk to God, sit in silence before God and listen. What daily practice can you commit to that will fill up your own oil? Biblically speaking, a lamp with oil includes a vessel filled with the illuminating light of the Holy Spirit in your life. So what do Holy Spirit–filled people do? They say no.

In his sermon, T. D. Jakes reminds us that sometimes the hardest word for us to tell a fool who is trying to drain our oil is *no*.[9] We think we can't say no to our bosses. We don't want to disappoint our parents. We are hesitant to tell our partners we can't pick up even one more load. We are scared to tell our children they've crossed a line. We don't want to hurt the people we go to church with. And so, over and over, we allow the people around us to take all of our oil, and eventually the very Spirit we once had inside of us gives out. Wise servants persevere. They play the infinite game. They run a race they can sustain. They know their boundaries, and they know when to say no. Wise servants know their pace. Wise servants give when they can, but not when they will have nothing left for themselves. Wise virgins put the masks on their own mouths before they assist the person next to them.

You must pay attention to the signs that your spirit is being crushed beneath the weight of all that is required of you. You must pause and breathe and ask yourself, "How can I fill back up?"

"The Lord is near," my mentor said, "but you are a human being, and your body is reacting to the stress you're under."

If we don't take a collective pause, our anxiety will cripple us. When we don't stop to breathe, the strain of our relationships will cause us to snap, and we may be the next person to lose our mind at Costco because they're out of toilet paper. Please, for the love of yourself and your family, put the oxygen mask securely on your own face.

Before we go any further, before we talk about relational resilience or the beauty of reconciliation, before we even say to another person "I'll see you tomorrow," we must be wise with our today. I think the first word we all need to be able to say is no.

A no just may save your life.

Positive and Negative Face

As a communication professor, I want to let you in on a little secret: *no* can bring you into a deeper conversation with someone than *yes*. In the book *Start with No*, Jim Camp flipped everything I thought I knew about negotiation upside down. He wrote that the word *no* is gold when trying to deepen communication. Jim believes that the word *no* starts negotiation rather than ends it. You don't have to fear hearing it or saying it to someone else.[10]

Jim says it's important when communicating with others to give them permission to say no early. People need to feel in control. In communication theory, we say it is one of our two most basic human desires: our desire to be in control (which in communication we call *negative face*) and our desire to be viewed how we wish to be viewed (which we call *positive face*).

Typically, if someone explodes on you, it is because you have stepped on their positive or negative face. You have attacked (and sometimes we do this by accident) the core image they are trying to project of who they are or you have taken away their autonomy. A quick way to strengthen your relationships is to keep people's positive and negative faces intact. If you know someone wants to be viewed a certain way, why not affirm what you see in them? This is what good teachers do if they want their students to grow. If I see a student taking a great deal of initiative in my class, I tell them I see it. I tell them they are a fantastic student and I can't wait to see how they grow as the semester continues. If I notice something about the people around me, why would I not want to tell them they are a genuine person or an honest person or a down-to-earth person or a personable person? I don't think we should be afraid to tell people what they are. In fact, I think more of us need people around us who are willing to encourage us with what they see. Give people their positive face. It is one of our two basic human desires.

Sometimes people explode on us because we attack their positive face. They want to be seen as in charge, and somehow we belittle their role. They want to be seen as intelligent, and somehow we minimize the school where they earned their degree. It is helpful to know this because it will help you to identify why you are feeling so much anger rise up within yourself. Think about how you hope other people perceive you. What would be the best way, a way that doesn't destroy a relationship, to communicate a frustration with how someone may have stepped on your positive face?

We must be careful not to attack even when we feel attacked. That will get us nowhere. The reason no one wants to release a nuclear weapon is because it will destroy everything and the whole world burns. Likewise, be cautious not to detonate on your relationships, no matter how much someone deserves it. It doesn't help to be petty. You think it will, but then a few days later you are consumed with shame and guilt. Let them take the low road. You take the high one. They may have been careless with their words, which is why you must be careful with yours. Careless words don't warrant a careless response. The first rule of communication is that you can control only yourself. Words can be explosive. Handle them with caution.

And that brings us back to the power of no. A negative face is your desire to be autonomous or in control. Attacking someone's negative face is when you tell them to do something without giving them the choice to choose. It typically won't work. If I say to Seth, "Do the dishes," he probably won't, not because he is a bad husband but because he is a human being, and human beings rarely like to lose autonomy. It is one of our basic desires. A more effective communication choice may be for me to say, "Is there a time today that you could do the dishes?"

Now he is in control of when he does them, and I still achieve my objective, which is that the dishes are done. Be careful in your communication not to back people into a corner. They may lash out. Provide people with choices. If I said, "Can you do the dishes right now?" and he said, "No," I would say, "Is there a time today you think you can do them?" That first no is going to make him more receptive to a yes, because now he feels safe and in control. *No* doesn't have to be a bad word. It is what allows people to exert one of their two basic desires and helps them to maintain a negative face.

If it is my turn to do the dishes, I want Seth to allow me

autonomy in when I do them. It helps me feel like it is my choice to do the dishes, not his command. These tiny relational tweaks will save you so much energy arguing with people about chores and duties. Something I actually love is when Seth wants me to do something I haven't done, he will say, "How can we work together on this?" We will talk about the power of a question in chapter 9, but let me tell you, a well-constructed question can give you something even better than an answer; it can give you a conversation.

Nothing allows us to access the power of our negative face quite like telling someone else no. Sometimes I say no to my kids before I even hear what they are asking. I do it reflexively, because now I feel as if I'm in control. Sometimes people will say yes to simply get you to go away. They have no intention of doing what you've asked. But when someone says no, it reinforces security.

Have you ever said no to your kid and then suddenly said yes? It's because your first no allowed you to think and process clearly. Once you said it, you were able to fully hear what they were asking, and you realized it wasn't unreasonable. *No* can sometimes let you fully hear what someone else is presenting to you. You don't have to be afraid of saying no or hearing no. *No* is not destructive. *No* does not make you a monster. According to Jim Camp, *no* is where we should all start.

Let Them Go

Sometimes you must cut someone off. Once when I shared some of the unhealthy things I was experiencing in my relationship with my ex-fiancé, a Christian friend paraphrased Romans 5:20 for me: "Where sin abounds, grace abounds more." Beloved, that verse is about Jesus, not you, and Christians who encourage you to stay in a relationship that makes you sicker instead of healthier are not doing a good job of being Christ followers at all. That is spiritual abuse. It is not unchristian or unholy to tell someone no. *No* is simply being wise with your oil. *No* is putting the oxygen mask on your own face. *No* is how you can feel safe again.

I had a moment during my breakup with my ex-fiancé when I felt so much guilt. I felt if I wasn't there for him, no one would be. For me, the situation became so toxic I was eventually granted a restraining order. My dad was instrumental in walking me through my own boundaries. I found the more I disclosed about the truth of our unhealthy dynamic, the more secrets I realized I was carrying. I want to share with you something my dad said to me all those years ago that helped me better understand what I was experiencing.

"You aren't the bad person here," Dad said. "You communicated your boundaries. He isn't respecting them. It is the choices he has now made that have given you no other alternative but to end communication. You are simply respecting his choice."

That made so much sense to me. Sometimes we can carry burdens that aren't ours to lift. We can worry that by saying "no more," we are somehow bad friends or bad partners or bad children. But if you communicate a boundary in a relationship, and someone makes a choice to disrespect it, then you are simply respecting their choice to end the relationship.

You said, "I don't like when you do X. I am asking you to stop doing it."

If they continue, even after you have clearly communicated

your expectation, could it be time to respect their choice? Not every relationship is meant to be fought for. And a really good way to know which ones are is to pay attention to who isn't respecting your no. *No* is not a bad word, but it is wrong for people to make you feel bad for using it. The only way for a pattern to stop is if one of you chooses to break it. You can't control anyone else's communication. You can control only your own.

Jim Camp says that starting with no will allow you to prepare a better yes. I am going to intentionally ask you a question right now that you will have no choice but to say no to. Please read the following aloud:

Question: Can you control everything in your life?

Your answer: _____

Your saying that first no out loud should now provide your brain with the ability, on this next question, to give me a healthier, more meaningful yes. You have just exhibited your negative face. You have just told me no. Please read this next question aloud and write down your response in the blank.

Question: Are boundaries something that can keep your relationships healthy?

Your answer: _____

What might a healthy relationship boundary look like for you?

How would placing one in your relationship help you play the infinite game?

In the next chapter, Seth is going to talk about why you must start creating new experiences for yourself. He is going to show you how sometimes we stay stuck in bad relationships we shouldn't be in, not because we are stupid and not because we don't know any better, but because we have created a learned state of helplessness. I don't want you to just say yes to new experiences. We say yes all the time, so much so that our yes is often meaningless. Before you say yes to something new, I want you to learn how to say no to something draining. It turns out that allowing yourself to say no is the key to living a more meaningful yes.

• • • •

Iron sharpens iron, and one man sharpens another. (Prov. 27:17 ESV)

ENGAGE

- *Share a thing you may have to say no to.*
- *Have you ever had to walk away from a relationship? What were the circumstances?*
- *What can you do today or tomorrow spiritually to try to fill up your oil?*

CHAPTER 6

The Door Is Open

*Look on every exit as being an entrance
somewhere else.*

TOM STOPPARD

My (Seth) phone rang. Heather was on the other end of the line, and she sounded out of breath. At the time I was working down the road at the nearby university as a carpenter. Heather had taken the year off from teaching to be with our new baby.

"Seth, I accidentally locked the door to the house and London was inside. She was crying and so I didn't know what else to do . . . My phone was locked inside . . . and . . ."

My mind was wondering where this story was heading.

"What did you do?" I asked, nervous of her reply.

London, our daughter, was nine or ten months old. Heather was London's entire world; they were rarely separated. When London saw her mother on the other side of the window, she started to panic. London had severe separation anxiety as a baby. I barely got to hold her. She didn't like anyone to hold her except Heather. She screamed bloody murder if Heather left her sight. I remember going to pick her up from daycare and seeing that she wasn't in the room with the other kids. The teacher of the room had taken her to a staff meeting. She didn't dare leave London to tough it out with the aide like the other children in the room would have to do. London was over a year old by then, but she still required extra attention.

"I kicked a hole through the door," she said.

"You did what?" I asked.

She sounded nervous. "I kicked a hole in the back door. I didn't know what else to do. London was screaming and I didn't have my phone. So I just kicked in the door."

There is something powerful about a child's cry, isn't there? When a parent feels desperate, they will do whatever it takes to calm their child's fears. Where some parents walk out the door, others kick them down. Heather was going to get to our daughter one way or another. Doors are meant to keep us safe from all the bad people in life. They keep out cold air. They force us to ask for permission. Doors are supposed to provide a degree of protection between us and everybody else. Doors divide. They lock. They are a signal to us that there is a difference between the inside and the outside. They are strong and solid. Doors make us feel safe. But what happens when the very doors that are supposed to keep us safe do the opposite? Some doors protect us. But others lock us in. Whether or not the door is good depends on who is in there with us. What do your doors look like? Where one door can symbolize Christmas celebrations, birthday parties, and nights together at the dinner table, another can symbolize isolation, fear, and nights wrecked with trauma.

We Can't Just See It; We Have to Experience It

What happens behind our closed doors has great influence on the way we think about ourselves. Behind the closed door of grief can be the inability to ever feel whole again. Behind the closed door of pain, one can develop an increased sense of anxiousness and fear. Behind the closed door of sexual abuse, a child can cultivate a deep sense of distrust toward people into adulthood. Behind the closed door of poverty, a person can grow up without the ability to feel secure in having their basic needs met. Behind the closed door of loneliness, a person can develop depression and the inability to form new relationships. Yes, sometimes doors keep us safe. But sometimes doors lock us in. Charles Dickens said, "A very little key will open a very heavy door."[1]

In the book *The Body Keeps the Score*, Bessel A. van der Kolk talks about a study at the University of Colorado on dogs who were locked in cages.[2] Wanting to understand helplessness in what feels like a totally unethical experiment, dogs received painful electric shocks while being trapped in their locked cages. They called the condition "inescapable shock."

Van der Kolk wrote, "After administering several courses of electric shock, the researchers opened the doors of the cages and then shocked the dogs again. A group of control dogs who had never been shocked before immediately ran away, but the dogs who had earlier been subjected to inescapable shock made no attempt to flee, even when the door was wide open—they just lay there, whimpering."

What's interesting about this study is that repeated trauma of the same nature doesn't make the dog want to leave the harmful situation once the door is open, but rather it has the opposite effect on the animal. They become helpless.

Van der Kolk added, "The mere opportunity to escape does not necessarily make traumatized animals, or people, take the road to freedom. Like dogs, many traumatized people simply give up. Rather than risk experimenting with new options they stay stuck in the fear they know."[3]

We can learn so much from this research when it comes to the effects trauma has on our brain's ability to pull us out of potentially dangerous situations and say no to things. As Heather explained, there are people we have to say no to. But our repeated cycles of dysfunction may be the very reason why we can't seem to get it together at times. Through years of dysfunctional relationships, we may have shocked our system in ways that leave us helpless to change our circumstances. Trauma is powerful. And until we begin to understand how it has impacted our lives, we may live in a state of helplessness and fear without moving beyond certain doors to find our needed healing.

The good news is that the study doesn't end there. Want to know how they were able to get the dogs out of the cages? They had to teach the traumatized dogs that the door was open by repeatedly dragging them out of their cages so they could physically have a new experience. Even though the dogs could see the door was open, they had to experience what it felt like to go through it. Similarly, sometimes our seeing an open door is simply not enough. We must experience it. It may not be enough to see a job opening we think we would be happier at; we must experience it. It may not be enough to know we could go to dinner with our coworkers; we must experience it. It may not be enough to have a therapist's card in our wallet; we have to experience it. It may not be enough to see what God is doing for other people; we have to experience it for ourselves. Seeing open doors is not enough; experiencing them is what changes us.

This is life-changing information. The only way to show helpless dogs that they are in fact not helpless is for someone to drag them toward the open door and invite them into a new experience. They needed new positive, repetitive experiences before they would leave the harmful situation on their own.[4] This is why a healthy community is so important. Where one person may be the cause of repeated shock to our nervous system, another person may provide the hand pulling us out of our helpless state. Healthy relationships are the small keys Dickens talked about. Positive communities provide these tiny moments of hope that help us open our heavy doors. Trauma that is inflicted daily, whether it is a verbally abusive marriage or an unhealthy family dynamic, keeps us stuck in painful situations.

One reason why people can stay stuck in bad situations for so long is because of learned helplessness. Trauma doesn't always make us run. Sometimes it makes us stay. That is what fight, flight, freeze does. Heather will walk you through this more in the next chapter, but when we experience some type of threat, our brains will often want us to fight, run, or freeze. Some people's reaction to bad experiences is to freeze.

Repeated traumas such as molestation, physical abuse, verbal abuse, hunger, and prejudice can all short-circuit our ability to regulate our mood and appetite. They can affect our sleep and prevent us from reaching our highest potential for learning.[5] Trauma causes us to isolate rather than seek out help. It sucks us dry of the will to dream a better life for ourselves and gets us trapped inside our thoughts. Repetitive trauma is the catalyst for hopelessness. If you've suffered from some type of repetitive trauma, you may feel as if the doors of healing have been slammed shut. That healing is a door that everyone else has access to except you. But you can start to look at that door in a different way. Just as Heather said in the last chapter, we can change our perception of the word *no* just as we can change our perception of our doors. No is not always a bad thing, and a closed door is sometimes a blessing.

If you remember, in the beginning of this book, I wrote that everyone has two sides: the side they present others with and the side that is visible only when the doors of their homes are all shut. It's because we all have secrets. Moments of shame. Times where we feel so broken by other people's actions toward us or our own choices that our lives feel like one big lie. Humanity is suffering. We've all messed up.

The problem is that we haven't acknowledged the reason for our pain, but it's the same reason why we can get out of it. Each other. The threshold of our lives is marked by happy-versus-horrible relationships. Moving beyond one door and opening ourselves up to another is the tiny key that can open a very heavy door.

How Are Your Relationships Designed?

Researcher, professor, and author Don Norman explained in an interview that his desire to improve the everyday function of life was spurred by a trip to England. He couldn't figure out how to use the light switches or doors in a different country, so he wrote a book, *The Design of Everyday Things*.

Norman explained that if we continually get things wrong, such as pulling on a door when it should be pushed, it's because the vertical handles have instinctively told us to pull and not push. We are not dumb; the door is poorly designed. Norman explained that one of the key indicators as to whether a door is well designed or poorly designed is that an object should communicate its function without a sign telling you how to use it properly. If the door says "Push," it's because it has a poor design.

A door that should be pushed should have no vertical handles but rather a flat plate eliminating the option of pulling on it at all. This lets you know the only way to enter through the door is to push. A door with vertical handles is designed to make you want to pull. The door is wrong, your brain is right, but it doesn't feel like it. The second you start pulling on a door that says Push or pushing on a door that says Pull, you immediately look around to see if anyone saw you. It's embarrassing. It feels like something must be wrong with you, but the problem is the door's design.[6] And, interestingly, now any door that is difficult or confusing to use we have termed the Norman door after designer Don Norman.

Perhaps this is what happened to you. Maybe you have high doses of relational hurt. Your closest relationships are symbolic of the doors in your life. For years you've trained your brain to instinctively keep pulling, keep holding tightly on to some of your relationships, when, in reality, you should've pushed through them a long time ago. That's why you're still stuck. You've been pulling some of your relationships closer and closer to you, but they are poorly designed relationships. They are people you should not be pulling closer. That's why you're so embarrassed.

Everyone around you says, "What are you doing? Don't you see that person is a door you are supposed to push yourself out of? You are going to get hurt! Stop pulling closer what should be pushed out."

Your effort is right; it is the design that is wrong. Of course, you are pulling them closer. They aren't supposed to hurt you. The title we give to people shapes the type of relationship we expect to be in with them. Why shouldn't you be able to trust your parent? Why shouldn't you be able to trust your friend? Why shouldn't you be able to trust your coworker? Why shouldn't you be able to trust your partner? Why shouldn't you be able to trust church community? Everything about the design of the relationship tells your brain you should be able to. So you expend your energy pulling and pulling and pulling, but it leaves you exhausted, empty, and embarrassed.

But what if you aren't dumb? What if your brain has been tricked? Just as Heather struggled to know when to leave her ex-fiancé, all of us, if we are genuine people, will struggle to know when to cut someone out or move on. It is probably one of the hardest decisions we will ever make—knowing when to push someone out of your life whom you would really like to keep pulling in.

The problem with pulling, even when the door is open, is that it depletes your energy. It is hard to invest in a new relationship when you are so exhausted from your current ones. It is hard to attempt a new experience when you'd rather just sit and go numb. Heather is going to provide you with a little activity that can strengthen the design of your relationships. It is something that will help you take accountability of your role as a door in someone else's life. It will help you to ask yourself the right questions so you can improve the design of everyday things.

Friendship Rules Theory

I (Heather) would like to walk you through an activity designed for my interpersonal communication course. In communication we have a theory called "friendship rules," which says that all our friendships are held together by following various friendship rules.[7] Maybe a rule for you is that if someone talks about you, your friend should stand up for you or else you deem them a bad friend. Maybe a rule for you is that none of your friends should continue a relationship with your ex after a breakup. Maybe a rule is that if there is some type of gathering, you expect this friend to invite you if the get-together is with mutual friends.

We decide who our friends are based on whether they follow the rules of our friendship. Friendships are not obscure things we do not understand. We create subconscious rules for them. And you know we create rules, because the second someone breaks one, we suddenly decide they are bad people. But maybe that is poor design. Maybe that is our Norman door.

Who consciously takes the time to define the rules of the friendship—that people who keep the rules are good friends, and people who break the rules are bad friends? All of this is done without any thoughtful exchange with the people we care about to effectively design the relationship.

After I broke up with my ex-fiancé, a friend we'll call Jane went to dinner with him. She did not go with him romantically, but she did hang out with him a few times and hear his side of the story. I felt betrayed by this. I felt as if it was a rule in our friendship that, after a breakup, you comfort me and not my ex. I don't care how much you like chips and salsa, this is a line, and if you cross it, you are dead to me. Possibly this was dramatically too much, but I was twenty-two at the time.

I didn't talk to Jane for several years after this, and I never told her why I had cut her off. We reconnected again at a friend's wedding, and I finally shared why I had distanced myself from her. Jane was gracious and seemed to understand, but looking back I feel I made a mistake. Hanging out with my ex was a rule for me, but what if that wasn't a friendship rule for Jane? Technically my ex was her friend too. She may have felt as if she was simply being a neutral party in the aftermath. For me, I didn't want neutrality. I wanted her to take my side and not answer his phone calls. In my situation, I had to get a restraining order, so I found it almost dangerous to have my friends provide him with doors or access points into my life.

But do you know what I have since realized? I don't think I was ever honest with my friends about how bad the relationship was. Jane couldn't know what I had never disclosed. I expected her to fill in the blanks, and then I decided she was a bad person when she did it incorrectly. Because I never communicated any of this to Jane, we truly were never very close again, and I feel bad about that. Today's Heather would never end a relationship without an explanation. It's not fair and it's cowardly. Jane had been my friend since I was thirteen. And today she could be a number on my recent call list had I simply explained to her the rules I felt she had breached in our friendship. I have missed out on having another person in my circle because of my haste to not let anyone walk over me. I am sorry, Jane. That was poor design. That one is on me, not you.

All of this background is to set up the following activity.

What are some rules that are important to you in friendship? I want you to do the uncomfortable work of sharing them with your close friends. It's called communication. I want you to say, "Hey, I'm reading this book, and I was tasked to think about what friendship rules look like to me. Here is what I have written down. I want to share them with you, because I love you, and I thought it would be helpful in our relationship to know where the boundaries are. Here are the things that would cause me to question this friendship."

Show them the rules. Ask them to write their own, and then have a healthy, wonderful conversation and learn about what each of you values and why.

Maybe one of your rules sounds stupid to them. Let them tell you why. Maybe one of their rules sounds dramatic to you. Tell them why. We are always better when we know the rules each person is playing by. We can't subconsciously design relationships and then consciously terminate them when others aren't abiding by that design. Sometimes it's not that Jane is a bad friend; it's that you never clearly communicated what the rules of this friendship are and why. What if, instead of cutting off Jane, I had explained my thoughts, let her explain her actions, and then simply said, "Okay. I'll take some time to think on this. But I'll see you tomorrow"?

Start by writing down seven Friendship Rules:

1. _____

2. _____

3. _____

4. _____

5. _____

6. _____

7. _____

Opening a New Door

My (Seth) mother has been married to my stepfather, Terry, for over twenty years now, and to this day I have never called him Dad. Our relationship is on good terms, but my wife always looks at me when I address his birthday cards to Terry instead of Dad. She says, "Would it kill you to write 'Dad'?" It's not that I don't view him as a father figure at this point in life; it's that the word *Dad* itself evokes a negative emotion inside of me. And it's not just with Terry that I struggle to say that word.

My father-in-law, whom I see several times a week, gives me a hug every time I see him. He tells me that he loves me and has always been an encouragement. In the fifteen years that Heather and I have been together, he and I haven't had one argument that I can remember. And yet I have never called him Dad. In both relationships I frame my sentences in a way that allows me to avoid needing to say it. Internally I acknowledge that it's a little awkward at this point to not call either of them Dad.

For years, as a child, I pulled extremely hard on the door of relationship with Cecil. Afterward I felt as if I had nothing left to give to another father figure. Words are powerful, as Heather mentioned in the last chapter. We all have different words that arouse negative emotions inside us. For some, it's the word *Mom*, because she left when you were a kid. For others, it's a season, because it symbolizes a time when your life fell apart. Every November, even if I don't consciously remember that my brother died right before Thanksgiving, my body does. Just seeing leaves change color makes me irritable. That's how sensitive our brains are. That's how the body keeps score. Words are powerful. And they can also be triggers. For some, it's the name of a spouse or a significant other you thought you'd spend forever with, before forever ran out. And so we pull and pull and pull on the doors we were meant to push through.

Life is a house with many doors. And on the other side of every threshold is an invitation to do things differently. On the other side are birthday parties and celebrations, anniversaries and graduations, healing, hope, community, communion, tomorrow.

There are new experiences that are awaiting all of us. The life you deserve is on the other side of letting go. The life you'd like is on the other side of letting someone in. The door is open. I'd like to close by sharing with you a tweet by neuropsychologist Dr. Jen Wolkin: "Trauma changes the brain and so does healing."[8]

•   •   •   •

So Jesus again said to them, "Truly, truly, I say to you, I am the door of the sheep. All who came before me are thieves and robbers, but the sheep did not listen to them. I am the door. If anyone enters by me, he will be saved and will go in and out and find pasture. The thief comes only to steal and kill and destroy. I came that they may have life and have it abundantly. I am the good shepherd. The good shepherd lays down his life for the sheep." (John 10:7–11 ESV)

ENGAGE

- *What is a moment in your life when a door opened?*
- *What past door has made you feel as if all the other doors since are shut?*
- *Is there a door in your life that is opened to you that you haven't been able to walk through yet?*

CHAPTER 7

The Shutdown

You learn about fight or flight, but no one ever
mentions the third alliterative option—freeze.
Nina Malkin

When I (Heather) was twenty-two, Seth bought me a massage.
I can't remember the occasion, but I thought it was sweet, and
I had never had a professional massage before that wasn't done
on a track field. In college my coach gave sports massages. I had
horrible shin splints, which eventually made running excruciating. She would try to release the lactic acid buildup by pushing
down on my shins. They hurt to be touched, but she was trying
to free up the muscles that were aching from the pounding of
the track. We took ice baths after practice. It was one of the only
things that brought relief to my shins.

It had been a couple of years since I had run with any purpose, and so my legs were calmer, but I still had occasional flare-ups when I jogged. And so Seth, trying to be sweet, arranged my first professional massage.

I showed up and was greeted by an old man. He brought me into a back room and gave me a glass of water.

"Drink this," he said. "Quickly."

I thought this was strange, so I held the glass in my hand.

"It will loosen the muscles. Lubricate them," he said.

The masseuse had a European accent, but I couldn't detect where it was from. I drank the glass of water. I can still taste it. It had a metallic flavor. He told me to get undressed and to get on the table. He said he had placed a sheet on the massage table that I should drape over me. I felt uncomfortable. There was a sense in the pit of my stomach that I should leave, but I brushed it off.

I wondered if I was being overly dramatic as I undressed and draped the sheet over me. But there was something incredibly unassuming about the masseuse. He was much older, in his late sixties or early seventies. It seemed as though this was something he did in retirement. I waited for him to come into the room and kept my head down. To this day I only visit massage booths in the mall that are in public view. I haven't gone to a masseuse alone since this one time.

When I left the masseuse's office, I drove out of the parking lot in tears. I had been inappropriately touched. Even worse than what happened was how my body responded to it. I froze. I wish I could tell you that it was fight or flight. That I jumped up the second I realized something was wrong and slapped him in the face. I wish I could tell you that I ran out of there with nothing but my sheet. But I didn't. I just froze.

The fight-flight-freeze response is a reaction to stress. You sense danger, and your brain decides to do what is optimal for your survival. If you corner an animal, it will do one of three things: attack, run, or freeze. It is important to note this response happens physically when psychologically you experience fear. One of the things that happens is that your heart starts to beat faster.[1] This is how your body gets more oxygen to your major muscles. Your lungs may start to speed up as they try to deliver the oxygen to your bloodstream. When you freeze, you may literally hold your breath. Adrenaline starts pumping and cortisol gets released. Your blood starts to thicken. This is how your body tries to protect you from injury. Your brain even dampens the perception of the pain to protect you from an attack. People who freeze do so because their bodies become overwhelmed, so frightened with a feeling of powerlessness that their brains, in order to keep their bodies safe, tell them to play dead.[2] It is important to know that none of this is a conscious decision. All of this is primal. And it is also important to know that this is all your body's way of protecting you, not hurting you.

For example, some people who freeze report the benefits of doing so. They tend to have little memory of the trauma.[3] A student was in the middle of giving a speech and suddenly stopped talking, stood frozen in place for two minutes, and then just ran out of the room. Later she told me she'd had a sudden memory of an assault. Something another student said had triggered a memory she had frozen away for several years. She ran out of the class and went to her mother and told her what she had psychologically buried.

Freezing is more likely to occur if we feel it is our only option, have a history of past traumas, or feel an imbalance of power. I think that is what it was for me. I was much younger. I had never been in this situation before. I was in his shop. I also am unsure what he put into the water that he made me drink when I first entered. It is important to remember, whether you went through something that caused fight, flight, or freeze, that all these brain responses are just your body's way of keeping you alive. You survived. Should we feel shame for surviving?

A few years later I saw that the masseuse had been arrested. He had assaulted another woman. In fact, once it made the news, five other women came forward. That brought about quite a bit of shame. I stayed frozen long after I left his office. Had I said something, who knows how many other women would have been spared. He was convicted of sexual assault and sentenced to ninety days in jail and ninety days on tether, with five years' probation. The sentencing was extremely light due to his age and a medical condition.

I've spent the last decade since then speaking at high schools and colleges to women and young girls about what I experienced and this understanding of the freeze response. Afterward girls have gone to the authorities and reported their assault because I shared with them the shame that has sat on me for decades because I didn't. One woman had a similar story to mine, and the man lost his massage license (thank God). Of course, we are all just doing what we can to survive, and no one should feel shame for what someone else did to them. But if I could do that portion of my life over, I would have said something to someone the day that it happened. For years I was so ashamed that I froze like that. I have run over and over the situation in my head. The shame is lighter now, but the regret is still there.

The Stress

We are all just surviving. So many of us are frozen. Just as Seth shared with you in the last chapter from van der Kolk's *The Body Keeps the Score*, sometimes the shocks we received while still in our cages cause us not to move even after the door is opened.

"I am seeing a theme," I wrote on Twitter, "so I would like to take an informal poll."

I asked the question, What has COVID hurt more?

a. My relationships with people.
b. My physical health.
c. My relationship with church.
d. My mental health.[4]

Within an hour I had over a thousand responses. Fifty-eight percent said the greatest negative impact of COVID was not their physical well-being but their relational well-being. They were losing their relationships with others (29 percent) and their relationships within the church (29 percent). Naturally, the next highest category (36 percent) was their mental health. Only 4.9 percent of people said COVID was impacting them physically. We are losing people not just to death or disease or COVID. We are losing the people we love and the communities we cherish to masks or no masks, Republican or Democrat, pro-choice or pro-life, gun reform or open carry.

I heard from people who had lost their babies during the pandemic and weren't able to grieve with family. People who lost their jobs. People who were no longer speaking to their families. Dozens and dozens of emails poured in. Fight, flight, and freeze.

All the Different Ways We Cope

A short amount of stress and adrenaline can cause us to freeze, but what happens when we experience cortisol drops in our bloodstream for long periods of time? A constant release of stress over time can cause us to shut down and even kill brain cells. In one study, young rats were placed in a cage with two older rats for twenty-minute periods.[5] The older rats acted out aggressively toward the younger rats. When they were tested, the rats who experienced aggression for twenty minutes had cortisol levels six times higher than the rats that didn't. So basically it's Facebook, but the comment section. Look, I love social media. I teach it and I host a podcast called *Viral Jesus* in which I talk to Christians about how they can use their social powers for good. I am not the person to make the case that the internet is a monster inside your home. It has benefits—a lot of them—but I'd be lying if I didn't also acknowledge it does its fair share of cortisol raising.

If you are in the business of arguing complementarian/egalitarian, get ready to open the floodgates. I get letters monthly. People spend their emotional energy printing out my tweets and expounding on why I am a heretic. One time they even sent letters to the church Seth was pastoring. I have never been my husband's employee. I think they thought that would put a lid on me. But Seth tends to like me a lot and is far more defensive of me than I am of myself. All I am saying is that if someone tested my blood, I bet I'd score like one of those little rats. Cortisol level six.

The rats were tested to see their neural cell growth. The rats who experienced aggression did grow cells at the same rates as the other rats who didn't, but a week later the cells were markedly reduced. The stress the rats had experienced had killed the brain cells they had developed. Researchers also saw that stress decreased short-term memory in the brains of rats. I had more to say here, but I suddenly forgot where I was going with this. (See what I did there?)

I see this a lot with Seth. We have purchased trackers that we keep on his wallet and his keys, and we put a GPS app on his cell phone. Seth's short-term memory really struggles. We joke about it, but I imagine it is also incredibly frustrating to him. Seth described some of his trauma in the last chapter, but I want to focus on some of our bad coping strategies when we experience stressors and some communication practices we can try to implement instead. We will look at the freeze response and how it is there to protect us and how our relationships have the ability to thaw us out. It is honestly incredible how one night with people who love you can have you feeling like you can live your life again.

When your brain is exposed to a high-stress environment for a long period of time, psychologist Karen Young suggests our brain may shut itself down: "When the brain is constantly exposed to a toxic environment, it will shut down to protect itself from that environment. The brain continues working, but it's rate of growth slows right down, creating a vulnerability to anxiety, depression, and less resilience to stress."[6]

Some of us aren't stuck; we are shut down. If you feel as if you don't know how to get your work done, if you can't figure out how to exercise anymore, if you would like to go out with friends but can't find the energy to do it, you may not be lazy—you may be shut down. Seth and I have watched several seasons of Netflix shows in a two- or three-day span. I have had mounting work to do and yet watched five straight episodes on a streaming service because it feels good. My brain was protecting me by releasing a numbing agent that dulls the attacks that seemed to be all around me: the pain of broken relationships, the ache of church politics, the triggers of racial upheaval, the constant threat of the pandemic. All of this became more bearable the more my brain tried to dull it.

Escapism is the tendency to seek distraction and relief from unpleasant realities, especially by seeking entertainment or engaging in fantasy. Closing a social media app and then reopening it, only to close and reopen it again in 0.3 seconds is our brain's way of escaping from all the chaos surrounding us. You shouldn't beat yourself up. If we don't intentionally give our brains a way of dealing with the stress we experience, it will try to provide us with a solution. Sometimes that is all addiction is: a coping strategy that becomes compulsive. When we are in peace, we can fully relax and engage with the world around us, but when we are in shutdown, withdrawal feels so much safer.

As a communication person, one of the things I do to help my brain regain control is to say out loud, "Hey, you. Big girl! I know you are trying to protect me. I know you are providing me with this strategy to dull the pain. But I think we need to try something different." And then I insert whatever different coping strategy I would like to do.

I know it sounds stupid, but if you read my last book, *It's Not Your Turn*, you know the words we say are extremely important to how our brains respond. "The brain it turns out," clinicians Andrew Newberg (a neuroscientist) and Mark Waldman (a medical doctor) observed, "doesn't distinguish between fantasies and facts when it perceives a negative event. Instead, it assumes that a real danger exists in the world."[7]

The words we tell our brains matter. It becomes as real as the ground we are standing on. Our brains respond to our negative thoughts as if they are real threats. You can't just say, "I hate my life," and expect it to have no consequences on how you view yourself. You can't just say, "I hate people," and expect it to not create your very reality. You cannot just say, "I'll never trust anyone again." I know you are feeling dramatic, and it feels good to spew out what feels bad inside, but what if our words create our world? Your brain will hear you, and it will produce more negative thoughts for you to "rabbit hole" down. Therefore, I talk to my brain. I redirect the ole girl. I thank her for trying to help me but then redirect her to a strategy I think may be more helpful. When I do this, I reduce my cortisol. I regain control. And you can too.

When I don't try to actively give my brain something to help me cope, it will probably come up with something for me, and I may not like it. So now I'm doom scrolling. Or binge eating. Or watching shows I will never admit watching to anyone because one of you will photocopy this page and send Seth an email.

For Seth and me, positive coping strategies look like talking. On some days Seth will say, "Hold me for twenty seconds" (the amount of time it takes our bodies to release oxytocin[8]). I know that sounds awkward, and maybe it is, but every time I squeeze him tight, both of us experience a biological response. That is because oxytocin can reduce stress, improve social bonding, and even reduce blood pressure.[9] And hugs, among other things, can release oxytocin. Something as simple as a hug can reduce our chances of getting sick.[10]

Emily Ho, a professor in the College of Public Health and Human Sciences at Oregon State University, recommends four hugs per day for survival, eight hugs per day for maintenance, and twelve hugs per day for growth.[11] How many hugs are you getting per day? I think about this for my single friends who go home alone at night. Women I know well, who have confided in me that they feel deprived of touch, I make sure to hug regularly. People need touch and affection. Unmarried people need touch and affection. Children need touch and affection. I plan to grow my family and loved ones one hug at a time. Even playing with your dog can increase your oxytocin levels.[12]

Spending quality time with loved ones can increase our oxytocin as well. If you are stressed, it is healthy for you to take a break from work and responsibility and go out to eat with someone you enjoy being with. The bonding, the laughter, the face-to-face brain chemistry, all increase oxytocin. Telling people how we feel, though awkward and scary, can leave us feeling more connected. Some other good coping skills you can try when you want to numb or resort to a bad strategy is a biblical practice such as meditation. If you live near a family member, try giving them a hug. If you have a dog, try giving them some extra attention. If you can spend time with friends, get out there and do it. The thing about human beings is we are wired to exist in social relationships. Our bodies reward us for being social. I know it is often the last thing you want to do when you are stressed, but I promise you it is what we actually need—each other.

Seth and I also do a lot of walking as a coping strategy. Our entire neighborhood should be able to tell how our work or family life is going. The more times we circle the block, the more you should be concerned. Seth loves being in nature. It's a coping strategy for him. He feels more connected to himself when he is hiking. Playing music is also a healthy coping strategy. If you are feeling overwhelmed, take a second and play "Take Me to the King" by gospel singer Tamela Mann or her song "God Provides." You'll feel yourself relaxing within a single verse. I also walk and say Bible verses out loud over my life. I repeat the Word of God back to God and ask for heaven's involvement. I say, "Lord, you said this first."

I have had many moments when a student is crying in my office, and I say, "Let's go," and we walk around the campus and repeat the Word of God over the situation. I do this because, as I told you earlier, words change our brains and our words can create our worlds. The words we tell ourselves become as real as the ground we are standing on. I want the promises of Scripture to be the foundation of my life. My walking with a student and processing with them could be the difference in their brain between shutdown or awakened. When you are sad, you will want to watch a show or play a video game, anything to dull and shut down the feelings you don't want to feel right now. But what we need is to call our Scarlett, or our Natasha, and ask if they want to sit and not move in front of *Lord of the Rings* for a while. We need social support. It's what helps us exit the shutdown.

You Need Someone

We could die without each other. Sounds extreme, but it doesn't make it less true. In 1995 Charles Sell offered some of the most heartbreaking research on the absence of parental affection.[13] René Spitz had recorded the growth of ninety-seven children in a South American orphanage who were deprived of relationship. There was enough staff to feed and change children ranging in ages from three months to three years old, but not enough staff funding to provide the emotional and physical support that a parent figure would. Again, basic needs were met, such as food, shelter, and baths. But emotional and physical contact could not be provided due to resources. No one was there to hold and cuddle the children. There was no one to sit babies on their knees and whisper sweet words in their ears. And apparently, we need that. In just three months the children started to show signs of deterioration.

Sell reported, "Besides a loss of appetite and inability to sleep well, many of the children lay with vacant expressions in their eyes. After five months, serious deterioration set in. They lay whimpering, with troubled and twisted faces. Often, when a doctor or nurse would pick up an infant, it would scream in terror."

Twenty-seven of the children died within the first year. That is almost one-third of these otherwise healthy children who deteriorated to the point of death. And it wasn't because they didn't have food or water. They died because they didn't have relationship. They died because they weren't experiencing touch and affection. They died because human beings need each other. We are social creatures. Seven more children died in the second year, and eventually only twenty-one children survived the ordeal, but even those who did had deep psychological trauma.[14]

We don't just *want* relationships with others. I am not just being poetic when I say you need your person or metaphorical when I say to find your team. Human beings were created to exist in relationship with other people. My best friend, Scarlett, always says, "You don't need a tribe." We don't need a flock of people dropping casseroles off at our doorstep in order to know we are loved. But there must be some middle ground between isolated and frat house pledge. We each need to find it.

According to a University of Minnesota article that looked at a study of a hundred people, scientists found that after going through a stressful task, they recovered faster when they were reminded of the people they had strong bonds with.[15] People are 50 percent less likely to die prematurely when they have strong social ties. Interestingly, people who feel they have deep ties with family and friends are also more satisfied with their health than people who report having hostility in relationships.[16]

A National Bureau of Economic Research surveyed more than five thousand people and discovered that good relationships make us feel richer. Loneliness is the same to our health as smoking fifteen cigarettes a day.[17] It can shorten one's lifespan by fifteen years. Yet, today, 47 percent of adults feel alone. And according to *Scientific American*, the United States has reached another boiling point: loneliness is everywhere. Doubling one's friend group has the same benefits to one's well-being as a 50 percent increase in income. So we may be poor in wallet, but stick with me and we shall be rich in spirit.

What we need in order to fight back against the creeping sense of dread is each other. We need to experience cohesion. Human beings thrive in environments where trust can be fostered and safety can be reached. We can truly save a life just by reaching out to our neighbors or stopping by someone's office for lunch. Deciding to prioritize the people around us can make a world of difference to someone whose world is shrinking.

Plato's Soul Mates

Symposium was one of the ancient philosopher Plato's most well-known works.[18] In it, he tells a story of how human beings found joy and sorrow. In the tale, Plato says that human beings were originally two people joined together. Each person had four hands, four legs, and two faces. They were powerful creatures that roamed the earth, and the gods became jealous. In a quest to weaken the human species, Zeus, the king of the gods, cut each creature into two halves. The broken humans were miserable. They walked the earth in devastation, searching for their missing halves. Each half was born with the innate desire to be fully whole and fully known, to heal the severed wounds of brokenness by reconnecting with their matching piece. And every now and then, one lucky soul would find another. And the two halves could heal their severed wounds and become whole. This is where we get the idea of soul mates. Two human beings waiting to find their other half, waiting to be made whole.

That leads us to ask, What is love biologically?

Love really is a lot less poetic than that, but if you like nerd stuff, let's dip our toes in. There are a bunch of hormones that create attachment bonds that make us feel love. Hormones such as oxytocin, vasopressin, dopamine, and testosterone, just to name a few. We see these hormones bond parents to children, and they also show up when you see a bond between two adults. Things such as physical touch can activate the body to produce these hormones as well. Sex can produce hormones that make you feel more attachment to your partner, but the thing about love is that it really isn't based on sex at all. Spending time together, cuddling, positive social connection—all of these increase various hormonal reactions that increase a couple's bond. They tell our bodies that we feel close to someone.

What is fascinating is that the hormones we see the body experience in parent-child relationships are the same hormones humans experience in romantic partnership, "despite some specific hormones brought about by sexual behavior."[19] Though it feels different in the way we describe them, the attachment bonds are produced by the same chemicals. "The myth that romantic love is essentially (biologically) different from other types of strong attachment is created and maintained by cultural beliefs and our world views, not our biology."[20]

We can experience deep emotional bonding and pairing in a variety of different ways as human beings, and the emotion we call love can be experienced in totally different ways too. Two friends are capable of pairing, even if there is nothing sexual happening. Church communities and familial bonds can also create these hormones biologically.[21] Maybe Plato wasn't all wrong. Maybe human beings need other human beings to feel fully whole.

Here is where I need you to take our study notes and apply it to your life. This is not a drill. There is more than one way to experience love. Romantic love is beautiful, but biologically you don't need a romantic partner to be in love with someone. It is only because of social and cultural norms that we believe romantic love is the main way to enter a loving bond, but the truth is there is so much more available to human beings than just romantic relationships. Humans need connection, and the beauty of this is that even if you never find your romantic partner, you are still very capable of experiencing a deeply loving relationship. You don't need to have sex to have a soul mate. You don't need to get married to be fully known. Our friendships and communities can stimulate your brain in the exact same ways. Love isn't a private affair for the few. It could be an invitation to the many. The hormonal process is the same, whether sex is involved or not.

I deeply love my friends. My friend Scarlett is one of my soul mates. I have known her for more than fifteen years. She has seen the best and the worst of me and always accepted me as I am. Vimbo, Tiffany, Cortney, my sister, and my parents. All of these people make me more whole. I love Seth deeply and romantically, but I am so grateful he is not my only shot at love. It is possible for someone to be single and live happily ever after if they find other outlets for their pair bonding to take place.

We have a variety of images that may pop into our minds when we think about love, but love is a bond with someone you have joy with and who you trust, mixed with a ton of different hormones that produce the things you physically feel. Again, the words we use matter, and I assure you there are people using the word *love* to gloss over relationships that have nothing of what love is. You can have a marriage, but that doesn't mean you have love. You can be single and yet be surrounded by it. Love is so much more than romance. It's stronger than kisses and butterflies. Plato was on to something. Maybe loneliness is the severing of how we were created. Perhaps isolation is the wound that only partnership can heal. Love, true love, is when your soul stops wandering. Because when you are with these other people, you finally feel at home.

If our feet are tired and our brains are numb from all the chaos that have overwhelmed our sensory systems, I'd like to suggest that we don't have to keep going on like this. We can find love right here, just as we are. We can find our missing pieces.

What if what we need to release us from this collective feeling of being stuck are people we can call our home? And what if we all feel lost because we have lost each other? In that South American orphanage, René Spitz discovered that we would die without each other. Plato thought philosophically that the human experience is one of such deep intimacy that we would wander the earth in mourning until we found what would make us whole.

Relationships unfreeze us. In the areas of our life where we feel stuck, love is the antidote. Often, the first thing we want to quit when we feel overwhelmed is the thing that we most deeply need. Put down your phone and stop scrolling. Turn off Netflix and unplug the video games. There is no need to feel shame. Your brain is simply trying to protect you. It is trying to dampen the pain sensors you may be experiencing. If we don't give our brain something to help us cope, it will choose something for us, and we may not like it. So thank your brain for assisting you, but when you are ready, there is a more fulfilling journey ahead.

Love, social support, oxytocin, and hugs are all better ways to pursue wholeness. Good relationships make all of us richer. The earth is filled with soul mates. And they don't have to be romantic partners. They can just be precious people who make life feel worth living. This world is aching with loneliness. Everywhere you look, someone is frozen. You don't have to go far before you realize someone else is stuck. Your life has a purpose. What if you aren't just a person? What if you are a plan? It isn't just about who can make you feel less lonely; it must also be about who *you* can make feel more connected. You may be the answer to someone else's plea. What if someone right now is wandering, and you could make them feel whole? What if the thing you most want to quit is the very thing you most deeply need?

• • • •

As a prisoner for the Lord, then, I urge you to live a life worthy of the calling you have received. Be completely humble and gentle; be patient, bearing with one another in love. Make every effort to keep the unity of the Spirit through the bond of peace. There is one body and one Spirit, just as you were called to one hope when you were called; one Lord, one faith, one baptism; one God and Father of all, who is over all and through all and in all. (Eph. 4:1–6)

ENGAGE

- *In what areas does your life feel frozen?*
- *Share a time in your life when you felt lonely.*
- *What is one thing you can do today to help foster genuine connection with someone? Send a text, write a message, make a call, visit with a neighbor.*

CHAPTER 8

Don't Miss Your Mark

Childhood is the one story that stands by itself in every soul.

IVAN DOIG

In 2013, I (Seth) made the journey back to college for what seemed the millionth time. I remember sitting in one of my undergraduate religion courses with my professor Glenn Russell.

"There really isn't much of a difference is there?" he said.

Not sure of his point, I became attentive. His eyes were calm and his voice was slow as he held out his left hand and said, "These are the sinners," and then raising his right hand a few inches higher than his left, "and these are the saints." Pausing for a minute, he raised his head upward, "There really isn't much of a difference when heaven is the mark."

His point pierced me. I always felt behind the mark. Without

Jesus, there isn't a difference between the sinner and the saint. His hands bear our mark.

Strike 1: Our Childhood

As a child I went on a visitation to see my dad when I was nine. My mother dropped us off at a Burger King for breakfast with him before spending a couple of hours at his new place. As my mom and Cecil made the transaction of swapping my brothers and me, I heard Cecil say he didn't have any money to buy us a one-dollar breakfast sandwich. In frustration, my mother handed him a twenty-dollar bill. After our meal we all crammed in the front seat of his truck and headed to his place. That's when I noticed on the dashboard an unopened box of cigarettes. A twelve pack. Even as a nine-year-old I knew those weren't cheap. I became instantly saddened because, though I was a child, I knew my father had prioritized his nicotine addiction over buying us breakfast for our once-a-month visitation.

For my eleventh birthday I wanted nothing more than to win my father's affection. I wanted him to choose me over his addiction, even if it was just for an hour. During my summer visitation, I noticed he had been absent for a while again. I found him in the garage with a beer in one hand and a clenched fist full of weed in the other. Anxious for his affection, I slowly tiptoed over to him. He picked me up and sat me on the counter. Pulling out a Marlboro Red from his pocket, he pressed it between my lips and lit it.

This was the only time during my entire childhood I can remember feeling accepted and even wanted by my father.

He smiled and said, "Next year I'll let you try the good stuff."

I felt special because Cecil and I shared a secret that my brothers didn't know about. While Tyler and Coty played video games in the basement, it became our custom to smoke cigarettes together over the next several weeks while he got high. He would often wink at me, and I would go into the bathroom and wait for the cigarette to be slipped under the door. Our "special" relationship faded after that summer, and my father's addictions landed him in prison for the next several years. He would spend much of my adolescence in and out of prison.

So much of life has been predetermined for us before we ever took a breath outside the womb. We had no choice who our parents were, what our socioeconomic status would be, if there were going to be groceries in the fridge, what neighborhood we would grow up in, if our parents were drug addicts, or whether or not we would be physically and psychologically harmed as a kid.

Think of the things that were out of your control when you were growing up and how they impacted your relationships now that you're an adult. Maybe for you it wasn't an absent parent. Maybe it was being bullied at school. Maybe it was shame over your body or your face or your sexuality. Maybe for you it was a learning disability. Maybe you were the only minority in your class. I don't know what it was that made you feel like an outsider looking in, but I do know that the experiences of our childhood become the echo of our adulthood.

Strike 2: Our Adolescence

As a high school sophomore I found myself struggling for a sense of belonging, feeling as if I had no identity due to poor grades and a scrawny build. That's when I decided to smoke pot in the bathroom of the private school where my mother taught. It only took about forty-five minutes for the news to reach my mom. Before I knew it, I could hear her screams echoing down the hallway as my name was called over the loudspeaker.

Finding myself expelled from school for the rest of the semester, I had nothing to do but examine my choices. I had never been a religious type until then. In fact, I didn't want anything to do with God or spirituality altogether. I couldn't trust God.

At that time I wonder if my distrust of people was partly due to my distrust in God.

Now that I am older, I can see that God didn't cause Cecil to make those choices. Cecil made those choices on his own. What God did do was see the unwillingness of a man's heart to change. The only thing worse than being from a broken home was staying in one. God didn't cause my pain, but he did redeem it. What I didn't realize at the time was that my pot smoking was an attempt to connect with Cecil. I truly thought that when he found out about what I had done, he would call me. He would be "proud" of me. All of this was a misconstrued belief. When he didn't call, it felt as if I didn't have anything left. Not even misplaced hope.

That's when I opened my Bible for the first time without being told to. Flipping open the pages of this ancient book I landed on Romans 8:15: "The Spirit you received does not make you slaves, so that you live in fear again; rather, the Spirit you received brought about your adoption to sonship. And by him we cry, 'Abba, Father.'"

It was on a cold floor in an empty house that I got down on my knees for the first time in my life and asked if God would be my Father. I was sick of this feeling in my stomach that wouldn't go away. I was sick of feeling abandoned. I wanted to be adopted into sonship.

In his commentary on the book of Romans, F. F. Bruce wrote about this verse, "The term 'adoption' may have a somewhat artificial sound in our ears; but in the Roman world of the first century AD an adopted son was a son deliberately chosen by his adoptive father to perpetuate his name and inherit his estate; he was no whit inferior in status to a son born in the ordinary course of nature, and might well enjoy the father's affection more fully and reproduce the father's character more worthily."[1]

Bruce is telling us that our adoption into the family of Christ has never relied on our family of origin. We are his because he looked at us in our abandonment and saw value. It's as if God intentionally overlooked the rules of birthright and birth order and chose us anyway. He saw in each of us the perfect fit to inherit his presence, as if we are in no way inferior to those who are next in line. To be adopted by God is to truly understand that no matter what amount of rejection we have experienced in our lives, he still sees us as the perfect fit to call his "sons and daughters." The apostle Paul added, "I will be a Father to you, and you will be my sons and daughters, says the Lord Almighty" (2 Cor. 6:18).

This is powerful for a world in need of secure attachment—fighting to make sense of rejection and moving forward. I tweeted once, "I got kicked out for smoking pot in the gym bathroom of my private Christian high school. I wasn't looking for God. In fact, I was mad at him. But God came looking for me . . . the pot head. We see pot heads. God sees pastors."[2]

Strike 3: Adulthood

I've worn a lot of hats these past five years, and many of them resemble those of a public servant—working with at-risk youth in public schools, setting up food resources for the community, teaching and preaching, and sitting by the bedsides of people in their last moments of life, to name a few. I have given a lot of myself to the people whom I deeply care about, and if I can be honest, I am a little exhausted. And by exhausted, I mean burned out.

Life has demanded so much of me these past few years, it has been hard to keep up with all of the sudden shifts that have taken place. I've realized we can give so much of ourselves to all the good causes in life that we don't have any life left in us. While we were writing this book, Heather had the opportunity to take back her old teaching job in Michigan on extremely short notice. It would allow us to be close to her parents, something we felt was very much needed. I said yes because I was mentally about to crash into a brick wall. I wasn't taking good care of my emotional and physical health while pastoring, and it was giving me a high level of compassion fatigue. I was on the verge of pastoral burnout in just a few short years.

We put our house in Colorado on the market, packed up all our belongings, and in less than thirty days we were home. Moving back to Michigan was the best thing I could have done for my family. Life is slower here, and I need slower. I had promised myself the year before that I was going to get some counseling to help me process a few things that were still bothering me, but I never made good on that promise. I even preached a short sermon series on mental health and said from the pulpit,

"I'll be the first one to call," holding up a business card with the name of a therapist. I didn't.

Michigan life has given me time to think about all those unresolved sore spots in my life again, except this time there are no more meetings to run to or late-night phone calls from church members in crisis to keep me from facing my own. It's easy to be the hero. It makes me feel important. It's comfortable to feel big. But we can't heal what we won't admit is broken.

What I've learned is that there is a great price to pay for our heroic acts of self-sacrifice, even if it is for the cause of the gospel. Heather told me of a podcast she did with Steve Cuss, the host of the *Managing Leadership Anxiety* podcast, and he asked, "How can I be fully attentive to others if I am not fully attentive to myself?"[3] He explained that if we aren't analyzing our own motives, we won't realize when we are projecting them onto others.

We can't blame everything on our past traumas. The reality is that we can dwell in the past as much as we want, but it won't change anything. Yesterday changes how we experience today, but it doesn't determine it. We can change. We can do things differently. In the next chapter, Heather is going to walk us through why change is so hard and why it is necessary. But even with my knowing all those statistics, I still struggled to make changes in my life. Michigan has helped me to make some necessary changes. Slowing down and not being a hero has revealed that I needed saving.

I wrote a lot of what I have shared with you from my in-laws' basement. When we moved, I thought surely God would provide us with the perfect home immediately. After all, he spoke and we obeyed. But then we made five offers on houses before finally being able to buy one. And the one we bought required a lot of renovation. We will talk about that in a later chapter.

My point is that for months I was a thirty-four-year-old man whispering to my wife at night. We slept right below her parents' bedroom vents. If that sounds romantic, I assure you it wasn't.

I never felt so unimportant. I had to really analyze with God what makes me feel like me. And I didn't want the answer to that question to be a job or a title or a house. I wanted to know who Seth was, even stripped from those things. Who was I when my phone stopped ringing? Who was I without someone else's conflict to focus on? My email in-box wasn't flooded. No one was asking how soon I could be somewhere. No one was asking me anything at all. It is hard to feel big in a basement. Without the things that I would typically allow to distract me, I was able to realize how much I loved being distracted. I wrote a lot of the stories in this book in spaces that made me feel really small. And do you know what I found? God was with me as much in the basement as he was in the pulpit. Maybe even more so.

I don't know what is making you feel small right now. I don't know what basement you are in. I don't know what has stopped moving around you just long enough for you to realize that you can't save yourself. *We can't save ourselves.* God doesn't need us to feel big; he needs us to recognize that we are small. What if these moments of insecurity are exactly what we need to be able to finally say, "Help me"? What if healing starts in the basement?

At what point do I stop blaming things on Cecil? At what point do I give him the grace I so desperately need for myself? At what point do I stop counting the strikes? Your past doesn't get the final word on your future. Our adoption into the family of Christ has the power to change every one of our lives. God gets the final word. His grace is enough. For Cecil, for me, for your divorce, for your addiction, for your anger, for your bitterness, for your grief, for your shame.

After all, "Here are the sinners," Dr. Russell said that day in class. And then raising one hand a little higher than the other, he added, "and here are the saints." When it comes to reaching heaven, none of us can make up the distance. Thank God, in the hands of Christ is our every mark.

The Ten ACEs of Trauma

Trigger warning: What I am going to ask you to do next may evoke strong emotions as you go through a series of ten questions scoring your own adverse childhood experiences (ACEs). You will add them up to see how certain areas of your childhood have impacted you in your adult life. So, if you're ready, consider delving into the influence your childhood has had on your present. In the following assessment, as you walk through each question and discover your ACE score, you will develop a better sense of self-awareness.[4]

The ten adverse childhood experiences (ACEs) of trauma typically include physical abuse, sexual abuse, emotional abuse, physical neglect, emotional neglect, mental illness, divorce, substance abuse, violence against your mother, and a relative who has been incarcerated.[5]

The higher your ACE score, the stronger the correlation between certain chronic diseases you can develop as an adult as well as "social and emotional problems."[6] If you score four or more, it puts your health and overall well-being at much higher risk. According to the American Society for the Positive Care of Children, certain diseases such as pulmonary lung disease increased 390 percent, hepatitis 240 percent, depression 460 percent, and suicide 1,220 percent.[7] The sooner you can clearly define the areas of adverse childhood experiences in your life, the sooner you can find healing. You can't heal what you don't know is broken.

The ACE Questionnaire
While you were growing up, during your first 18 years of life[8]

Did a parent or other adult in the household often or very often . . . swear at you, insult you, put you down, or humiliate you, or act in a way that made you afraid that you might be physically hurt?
Yes
No

Did a parent or other adult in the household often or very often . . . push, grab, slap, or throw something at you, or ever hit you so hard that you had marks or were injured?
Yes
No

Did an adult or person at least five years older than you ever . . . touch or fondle you or have you touch their body in a sexual way, or attempt or actually have oral, anal, or vaginal intercourse with you?
Yes
No

Did you often or very often feel that . . . no one in your family loved you or thought you were important or special, or your family didn't look out for each other, feel close to each other, or support each other?

Yes

No

Did you often or very often feel that . . . you didn't have enough to eat, had to wear dirty clothes, and had no one to protect you, or your parents were too drunk or high to take care of you or take you to the doctor if you needed it?

Yes

No

Were your parents ever separated or divorced?

Yes

No

Was your mother or stepmother often or very often pushed, grabbed, slapped, or had something thrown at her or sometimes, often, or very often kicked, bitten, hit with a fist, or hit with something hard or ever repeatedly hit at least a few minutes or threatened with a gun or knife?

Yes

No

Did you live with anyone who was a problem drinker or alcoholic or who used street drugs?

Yes

No

Was a household member depressed or mentally ill or did a household member attempt suicide?

Yes

No

Did a household member go to prison?

Yes

No

Each "yes" is one point.

SCORE TOTAL _____

Note: If after taking this test you have opened some wounds that need further exploration and restoration, I recommend looking for a therapist in your area who deals with childhood trauma. Some book resources I have found helpful in my own journey toward healing include the following:

- Bessel A. van der Kolk, *The Body Keeps the Score: Brain, Mind, and Body in the Healing of Trauma*[9]
- Brené Brown, *Braving the Wilderness: The Quest for True Belonging and the Courage to Stand Alone*[10]
- Shannon Thomas, *Healing from Hidden Abuse: A Journey Through the Stages of Recovery from Psychological Abuse*[11]
- David Richo, *Daring to Trust: Opening Ourselves to Real Love and Intimacy*[12]
- James H. Cone, *The Cross and the Lynching Tree*[13] (for understanding the gruesomeness of our racial history and trauma but also for how we must keep thirsting for life and not let the worst determine our final meaning)

Some TED Talk resources include the following:

- Nadine Burke Harris, "How Childhood Trauma Affects Health Across a Lifetime"[14]
- Brené Brown, "The Power of Vulnerability"[15]

· · · ·

The Lord is close to the brokenhearted and saves those who are crushed in spirit. (Ps. 34:18)

ENGAGE

- *Can you see a correlation between one of your ACE scores and struggles you have now?*
- *From God's perspective, what's the difference between sinners and saints?*
- *Seventy percent of people have experienced trauma. How may this change the way we view the people who have hurt us?*

CHAPTER 9

Change to Live

Friends are the siblings God never gave us.
MENCIUS

My (Heather) mother was not supposed to be working that shift, but a friend asked if she would cover for her. The Broadway show *Jesus Christ Superstar* would be playing downtown that evening.

"Want to join us, Vicki?" she asked.

But my mom had already seen it. She didn't care to join, but she would cover her friend's shift. My mother was a waitress at a swanky restaurant in Grand Rapids, Michigan. The after-lunch-before-dinner shift was hardly lucrative. My dad, along with a coworker, came in and sat down at her table. If my father were telling this story, this is where he would talk about the one detail I have heard him say over and over my entire life.

"The moment she walked to the table, it was like the Holy Spirit whispered, 'That's her.'"

He leaned over to his friend and said, "That's my wife!"

His friend laughed and said, "Yah, Joel, sure it is."

My dad is black and my mom is white. Neither of them had ever been in an interracial relationship, and theirs would cause many challenges for them. My mother's parents did not attend their wedding. Their being together impacted the towns they lived in. They have been denied housing. My grandparents would not have a relationship with my parents until my sister and I were born. The grandparents I grew up knowing were very different from the people they had been. People can change. I know that personally. Grace belongs to both the sinner and the saint. I live today in that freedom. But racism is not a history book for my family; it is the pages we have lived, the stories that were told.

Growing up biracial has always caused me to see race from a unique perspective. I have black friends who, based on past trauma and experiences, view most white people as untrustworthy. That has never been an option for me. The most trustworthy woman in my life had a white face. But I also see quite clearly that combining power with privilege is a dangerous cup for any human to drink from. A fruit of the Holy Spirit is humility. The life of the Christian should be marked by it. I hear the cries of my black brothers and sisters with a very tuned ear. The earthly hands that have always held me most steadily were the hands of my father, the hands of a black man. For me, black is a symbol of strength, a symbol of safety.

As Seth said in the last chapter, at what point do we give the people who have hurt us the grace we so desperately need for ourselves? "Your past doesn't get the final word on your future," he wrote. My grandparents repented. Because of that, redemption was possible. And my life was so much richer because they chose to be in it. People do change. Patterns do break. Grace belongs to the people who don't deserve it. I don't want you to change out of fear of what you will lose; I invite you to change because of the joy you will find.

My dad was in Grand Rapids only a couple of days. He was visiting from New York City, touring with the show he was acting in that year: *Jesus Christ Superstar*. He played the character of Simon. He asked my mom if she wanted two tickets to the show. Suddenly she did. It didn't matter that she had seen it before. This time would feel new. My mother moved that same year to New York City. They have been married now for more than forty years. There are many days I have thought to myself that the only reason I exist is because my mother walked up to my dad's table. The only reason you can read this book now is because a friend of my mom didn't want to work her shift. Life is filled with small, tiny shifts.

In the last chapter, Seth walked you through grace. Grace for yourself and grace toward others. He reminded us that where we may see a problem, God sees a promise. In this chapter I want you to see what grace can bring you: hope. Your life, marked by grace, has hope around every corner. We have to start living again. This is why we must step out of the cages we've locked ourselves in that we learned about in chapter 6. The door to new experiences is always open, and it may look a lot more ordinary than you think. Sometimes picking up a shift will alter our entire lives. Hope is your traveling companion.

There is life to be lived from right where you are. There is promise available to us right in our present. That is the beauty of still being alive. The story twists at the flip of a page. In one small, otherwise ordinary moment a seed can be planted that changes everything. Every day becomes an opportunity. Every casual interaction becomes a new possibility. There is always hope for tomorrow because you have adventure available today.

Turning Ordinary Moments into Relationships

In 1984 Michael Jordan made his debut in the Olympics. He averaged seventeen points a game. In that same year, the rookie arrived in Chicago. He was new to the area and didn't know his way around.

He had been drafted third overall by the Bulls, but the star college athlete had yet to become a household name. In fact, he got off the plane and started looking for the car that was supposed to drive him to where he would be staying. It didn't show up, or at least he never found it. There were no paparazzi then. No fans rushing him in the hallways. No posters to sign or movie deals. The first game Jordan played in the Chicago area was in the preseason. It was in a high school gymnasium. The game wasn't even televised. The entire world was about to shift economically, technologically, and athletically. But no one knew that in 1984, on the day Michael Jordan met George Koehler.

George was a limousine driver. He couldn't find the fare he was supposed to pick up at the airport. Coincidentally, the new Chicago Bulls player couldn't find his ride.

"Are you Larry Jordan?" George asked, rolling down a window and looking at a six-foot-six Michael.

Larry was Michael's brother. The two were only eleven

months apart in age and grew up playing basketball together. When George saw Michael, he thought he was Larry. Larry takes some credit for Michael's commitment to the game. He says it was their childhood and teenage rivalry that made Michael great.

Larry probably isn't wrong. Serena Williams is the younger sibling of Venus Williams, who is also a well-known and respected tennis player. But Serena, who is fifteen months younger, dominated the sport shortly after her arrival on the scene. One of the more fascinating parts of sports science is called the "little sibling effect."[1]

Studies show that younger siblings have a significantly higher chance of becoming elite athletes, and the advantage seems to be apparent regardless of gender. In a 2014 study about soccer players, researchers found that only 5 percent of professional players are only children and only 20 percent are the oldest sibling.[2] Even when two siblings both go pro, it is typically the younger who excels in the sport. Again, even in things we think are totally independent of social ties, such as genetics and athletics, we see that our social worlds make us who we are.

Michael Jordan was the youngest of three sons, and in the ESPN documentary *The Last Dance*, he said, "I don't think, from a competitive standpoint, I would be here without the confrontations with my brother."[3]

Human beings do not operate outside of their connections to one another. Iron sharpens iron. Our relationships with the people around us have a significant impact on how we engage with the world. One of my favorite theories in communication is called Social Judgment Theory. It says essentially that our judgments are made socially. We like to think that we are independent of influences, but to be human is to be influenced.

Michael Jordan may be the legend, but you might not know his name today if it hadn't been for Larry.

George Koehler ended up giving Michael a ride to his hotel. He was paid twenty-five dollars. It was an ordinary exchange. People get rides all the time. We interact with new people every day. And had George not done what he did next, he might still be a limo driver.

"Hey, if you ever need anything in Chicago," George said, handing Michael his card, "or need to know where to go, just give me a call."[4]

Two days later Michael called George because he needed to know a good place to get a haircut. The two have been best friends ever since. And while Jordan reportedly keeps a small circle of intimate relationships, few are closer to him than George Koehler. George was a limo driver. And Michael was a rookie player who needed a ride to a hotel. Yet neither of them has ever been the same. All because they chose to embrace the ordinary moment that led to an extraordinary relationship. Every single person outside of your family of origin that you now love was at one time someone you did not know. And that is why life is so important to keep showing up to. It is filled with small, tiny shifts. Dots that, once connected, change everything.

Seed List

Students ask me all the time, "How do I make friends?" And whenever you wonder the same thing, I want you to remember the story of Michael Jordan and George Koehler. The chauffeur gave the rookie an invitation, and two days later the rookie acted on it. Of course, neither of them knew this small gesture would be what launched George into being Michael's best friend and personal assistant for the rest of his career. But rarely do we ever see such things coming. You won't ever see the fruit while staring at the seed. Seeds feel so insignificant. They are tiny, easy to lose, and take a lot of energy to transform. But if you want a fruitful life, you are going to have to plant some seeds.

If you were to throw yourself a birthday party this year, and money was no object, who would you invite? Someone pays for a caterer, musicians, and decorations. All you need to do is create a list. Whose name would you write down? At the end of this chapter, I am going to give you space to write down a minimum of five names you would invite to that party. This is not your guest list, but your seed list. Don't do it yet, because I want to take the next few minutes to alleviate some of the pressure you may be feeling about it. We are going to write down in these pages the five names of the people you would like to invite to your party. Maybe you'll truly throw yourself a birthday party this year and actually send out those invites. Or maybe you just start by asking these five people, individually, if they would like to meet up for coffee. It is time we start being intentional about our relationships. If five names for you is super easy, think of five names of people you know that may appreciate your invitation. If your life is already full, how do you make someone else's fuller? If you aren't lonely, I assure you, someone else is.

Some of the people you write down may not be available. That is okay. Remember, in communication, we recognize we can't control other people's behavior, but we can control our own. So take a deep breath and remember George Koehler's handing his card to Michael Jordan. Maybe they will call and maybe they won't, but what they do with their opportunities should never hinder what you do with yours. This is your relational health we are talking about. Remember what we learned in chapter 7: you are 50 percent less likely to die prematurely if you have positive relationships. And doubling your friend group has the same benefits to your well-being as a 50 percent increase in income.[5]

Do you want to bear fruit?

Then open your hand, raise it to God, and say,

Lord, help me to be faithful with these few seeds. May you multiply the relationships you have put in my hand. Give me strength and confidence to try new things and make new invitations. And give me the time and patience to notice those whose invitations I have ignored. Here are my seeds, Lord. Have your way. Amen.

Change or Die

I know putting yourself out there socially won't be easy. Our brains hate change.[6] When you were just the cutest little baby in the hospital nursery (I mean, seriously, you were stunning), your brain was made for change. You experienced new things all the time. This is how you figured out what patterns to form for yourself, based on the results to the behaviors you tested. The only problem is, eventually, your sweet, precious, cute little baby brain started to grow up. And now, no matter how many times you tell yourself you are going to do life differently, your brain, through no fault of your own, starts selecting pathways that allow it to operate automatically. So while I would like to eat a salad or drink a fruit smoothie with lots of kale for my lunch, here I am again at Chick-fil-A, and I swear this process was involuntary. Research has shown that our brains will tend to stick with what we know, even if it's not in our best interest, because the brain prefers to take a path that feels familiar. Even the apostle Paul confessed, "I do not understand what I do. For what I want to do I do not do, but what I hate I do" (Rom. 7:15). We know how he feels.

Neuropsychologist Sanam Hafeez would explain it to the apostle in this way: "The more you do something the more ingrained it becomes in neural pathways, much like how a computer that stores the sites you visit—when you log onto your browser, they will pop up because you use them a lot. Change is an upheaval of many things and the brain has to work to fit it into an existing framework."[7]

According to the Center for Creative Leadership, the reason 75 percent of change initiatives fail in any given company is not because the ideas are bad and not because change isn't needed; they fail because of resistant company culture.[8]

In the book *Change or Die*, Alan Deutschman revealed that the diet choices of a group of people were analyzed, and doctors told them they must change their exercise habits or they would die in less than a year. Ninety percent of them, rather than change their habits, died in less than a year.[9] Most people would rather die than change!

If you are trying to put yourself out there and make new friends, it may not come to you naturally. That doesn't mean you are bad at it, and it doesn't mean it is a sign you shouldn't be doing it. It just means your brain needs some more time to process the new pattern you are providing it. So simply tell that old goat, "Hey, brain, I know you are trying to keep me safe and take the path of least resistance here, but I must start doing some things differently. I am going to try something new. You will not like it, but it will be good for both of us."

And though your brain dislikes change, change is really good for it. Truly! Switching up your patterns can increase your memory and positively impact your creativity. Interestingly, change stimulates your hippocampus, which is the area of the brain where all your long-term memories are stored. That process allows you to experience your life with greater emotional depth and connection. If you want to start creating and producing positive memories, a great way to do that is to start thinking about what routine disruption you can do today to get your brain to start processing a bit differently. Take a different way home. If you usually text someone, call them. If you would typically pack a meal for lunch, today go out and buy one.

There are also brain sites, such as Lumosity and BrainTrain, that provide you with visual and spatial exercises that will help stimulate your brain. If you're frustrated by having to do something different, that's a sign that it is working. I know trying to put yourself out there, after everything you have been through, is not going to be easy. Again, 90 percent of people would rather die than change. But you aren't one of them. You are reading this book. You care about what is happening on this small planet. You are longing to make a difference. You were created to be a game changer.

I teach a class on persuasion. A very effective persuasive tactic is to scare people into action. Politicians do it all the time. Create the "other," create an enemy, and rally people behind fear. Scare people into believing immigrants will take their jobs. Scare people into voting for you because you are the only one who can stop this war. Scare Republicans away from Democrats and Democrats away from Republicans. Scare Christians away from non-Christians and make Christians the monster of the secular world.

Fear is an excellent motivator, and we all have rallied behind it. But fear is not the tactic I think any of us need. Our brains are stressed. They are overwhelmed and shutting down. I don't want you to change because you are afraid (though there are real and scary consequences to living your life alone); I want you to change because you've been inspired. I don't want you to change because you don't want to die; I want you to change because you want to live. The world will tell you change or die, but the Lord invites us to change to live.

The Strength of Weak Ties

Even though everyone who has watched the Netflix documentary *The Social Dilemma* has told you to shut down your social media, here is why I don't want you to shut it down: you need weak ties. Yes, we need close connections. Yes, we need deep, intimate relationships. Yes, Plato was especially striking the right chord when he said human beings are severed halves looking for their whole. But we need Carols too. Carol is my term for strangers on the internet who will gas you up six out of seven days of the week. (Carol needs a Sabbath.) I love Carols and their male counterparts who function in quite the same way. I call them Carls. I will stop scrolling to hit Like on Carol's dinner plans every single time. Do I know Carol? No. Have I ever had a Zoom call with Carl? Not yet. But people who go out of their way to show us kindness, who remember to circle back about a prayer request from last week, who ask you how your day is going, who laugh at your jokes deserve your mutual attention. Weak ties are valuable to your life.

Now, when I say "weak ties" I am referring to relationships with people who are more infrequent and casual. If you think of your social life as concentric circles, the inner ring would be your strong ties. These are lovers, family, best friends, or, in my case, Nancy at Hacienda who brings me a limitless supply of chips and green salsa. I love you, girl. But ask anyone who lives in a small town, and they can tell you about the strength of weak ties. You can walk into a diner alone and not be alone in a small town. These people may not be calling you to see what your plans are for Christmas, but when you sit in the booth, they notice that you came. They ask you where you've been. They ask about the job hunt, or the fishing trip, or the hospital stay. Small towns are filled with dozens and dozens of everyday ties. And all ties are vital to your relational well-being. Christianity should be the place where people who are lost get to hear their name and have someone smile that they came. Heaven is a small town.

Strong ties are where we spend most of our energy. We typically validate only these relationships and assume all our other relationships are a drain on the energy that could be going to these strong ties. But in 1973 a Stanford University sociology professor turned what you thought you knew on its head. Mark Granovetter wrote what is quite possibly the most influential paper on relational development ever seen in the social sciences. It was titled "The Strength of Weak Ties."[10]

We say things like "quality over quantity," and, yes, quality is incredibly important to your inner circle. But quantity can make you feel a sense of belonging too. So maybe you've been down on yourself because you have casual workplace relationships but are still missing that office pal who you can talk to about *Ted Lasso* on the company dime.

Look, I get it. I have a workplace best friend. Her name is Lynn. She is more than twenty-five years my senior, but the other day I was in my office and heard someone loudly singing down the hallway while playing a ukulele, and I smiled because I knew that was Lynn. I don't just go to work because I love my job and get to foster the next generation of young people. I also go to work because I know, at lunch, I can slam fried pickles with Lynn at the local watering hole and she will reach over my plate before I'm finished and ask if I'm taking my leftovers.

Lynn makes my workspace feel like my living room. She is incredibly important to my job, but the strength of weak ties says that even more important than having a Lynn is having dozens of Carols. Carols and Carls are not just online. They are in person too. They are the mail guy who I joke with every time he drops a package on my desk. They are the cashier at my Starbucks who says they love my hair today. It is Shirley at the diner I make sure to eat breakfast in at least once a week, because if I am gone too long, she will bring it up the next time she sees me. Our weak ties are incredibly valuable people to our well-being.

One day I was on Twitter and tried to explain to my social media community the beauty of Carol.[11] I said, "I teach social media. So many people do these apps all wrong. They only respond to people with big followings and ignore small accounts." Right in front of you are Carols and Carls everywhere who are showing you kindness and intentionality, and if you aren't careful, you'll miss it. Put some respect on Carol's name, and Carol will respect you.

I added, "If you want to grow your socials, be social. Chrissy Teigen will never love you like you love her. But Carol will like that tweet everyone else scrolled right past, so don't ignore her. Respect your audience and they will respect you."

Paying attention to Carol and Carl is not about getting likes; it is about the value of weak ties. It is about paying attention to people because they are people. It is about not asking what someone can do for you before you decide if they are worthy of your energy. It is about building a social framework. My students will tell me all about a friend who they haven't been able to lean on, and I always ask them, "So where can you lean?"

Sometimes we look more at what we don't have than at what we do have, and therein lies the difference between gratitude and disappointment. We see this clearly in the online world, but this is also true off-line: weak ties matter. Weak ties are what make most of our world go round. Who recommended you for the job that is keeping a roof over your head? We tend to think it is our close ties that provide us with new experiences, but it is our weak ones. Of 282 people surveyed who were Boston-based workers, guess how many of them had applied for their job based on a tip from a weak social tie? Eighty-four percent.[12] People who have large weak-tie networks tend to be happier overall. They also experience a greater sense of belonging. People who are a part of CrossFit or yoga or a rifle club, people who are in your church community or dance studio or cooking class, all these people make you happier. They make you feel secure. You need them.

The people you meet at your gym class, the coffee barista who always remembers your order, Nancy at Hacienda with the salsa, all these people matter, and all of them contribute to our greater well-being. I want you to know this because sometimes we don't attempt to form relationships because we are holding out for only the people with whom we think we can experience deep relational intimacy. But heaven is a small town. Every person is significant. We tend to want only soul mates and believe anything else is a waste of time. But you experience important relational satisfaction, not just from lovers and parents and best friends, but also from Carol and Carl. So put some respect on their names, and Carol and Carl will respect you.

By the way, after I tweeted, Chrissy Teigen responded to me.[13] She said, "I talk to everyone and I like everyone?" and then she followed me. So now Chrissy Teigen is one of my weak ties. And I am a Carol to her.

So don't shut down your social media. Loneliness is the same to your health as smoking fifteen cigarettes a day. It can shorten your lifespan by fifteen years.[14] Stop trying to be bougie and shut down Instagram because all the other millennials are doing it. Practice moderation, give your brain a better coping strategy for stress than scrolling every 0.3 seconds, but don't diminish your online friendships. They just may be getting you through. We need weak ties.

Developing Your Growth Beliefs

According to Marist Poll, 80 percent of Americans under thirty believe in soul mates.[15] Seventy-three percent of Americans agree with them. I bring this up because this idea doesn't just impact our romantic relationships. The American obsession with soul mates, I think, bleeds into how we view all other relationships. We are so focused on the strong ties that we miss the beauty of the weaker ones. I think the idea that we are going to find one person and live happily ever after has really made the process of relationships even more confusing.

Researcher C. Raymond Knee of the University of Houston looked at how our beliefs about soul mates impact our relationships.[16] He named two distinctive processes called "destiny beliefs" and "growth beliefs." Destiny beliefs tell us we are destined to be with a specific person—that is, a soul mate. Growth beliefs say relationships progress slowly. We grow to fit together, and love is something that can be built and takes effort to be maintained. When we have a destiny belief, we tend to ask, "Is this my person?" "Is this my soul mate?" "Have I finally found love?"

People who have growth beliefs ask questions such as "Are we a good fit together?" "Is there a way I can grow to be better?" "Can I make this relationship better?" The tension arises when destiny believers experience a dynamic in their relationship where one party disappoints the other. They immediately feel tricked. "This can't be a relationship worth investing in because something just went wrong. I don't want to work so hard at this." The frustration we experience during incompatible beliefs and experiences causes us to say, "Forget this. I'm going back to Hulu." It is like me crying to Seth because our friends didn't invite us to game night. Does this one negative incident really negate twenty-five positive ones?

People who have growth beliefs tend to seek solutions for relationship problems. They don't believe there is just one person you magically fit with. Because no one is a unicorn, they believe relationships are meant to make both parties bend a little. They see compromising strategies as growth experiences. What ends up happening, according to Knee, is that destiny believers are more likely to give up and break up when relationships get difficult. They assume a struggle means this is not the right person to experience any sort of intimacy with rather than adapt a growth mindset.

The reality is, no relationship will ever be perfect. This is not Carvana. This is another human being with a totally different brain map than you. I think it is helpful to find someone who you agree with on values, but to look for your carbon copy on all opinions, news sources, theological ideas, and interests is pretty narcissistic. There are things you are wrong about. There are things you are uptight about. There are things you are too conservative on. There are areas you may be too liberal with.

I didn't know if Seth was my soul mate until Seth put in the work with me to become my soul mate. He has become my greatest partner. He has truly made me a better person. He has made me more trusting, not less. He has made me more compassionate, not less. He has made me more grateful, not less. He has made me a better listener, a better Christian, and a better friend.

It is not that Seth is this incredible person who magically tamed the shrew. It's that the process of working out our differences with mutual respect, value, forgiveness, and love toward each other has transformed my approach to all my other relationships. I don't know if I believe in soul mates as a person, but I do believe in soul mates as a process. The process of give-and-take, of defer and hold your ground, of holding someone accountable and forgiveness just because has been incredibly beneficial to my character.

What if you aren't looking for a specific person as much as you are looking for a partner to undergo the relational process with? That is why we keep coming back to basketball in this book. You need someone who helps you with assists. You need someone who challenges you with drills. You need teammates who grow with you, not a soul mate who doesn't exist. You want to find a partner who helps you best navigate the process.

This process is something that will require you to give mutual respect and submission, loyalty and integrity, honor and compassion. How does this mindset change the relationships you value? Soul mate is not a destination; it is a journey.

Good Question

Now that you aren't looking only for relationships with people who are perfect, let's start planting seeds.

One day my brother called me. He was about to go on a date, and he was nervous, so he called his favorite communication professor.

"What if she doesn't think I'm interesting?" he said.

I think a lot of us struggle with this. We worry about how we should approach people because we don't know what we will say. We worry that we won't be funny enough, smart enough, fascinating enough. We see someone who is nice at work or school or church or the gym, and we just say hi because we have no idea how to make friends as adults. Our brains don't like change. We are overworked and underpaid. And while we would all love a Lynn of our own to play the ukulele with, we don't know where to start.

First, let me take all the pressure off. Communication is rarely about you. The goal is not to convince someone else that you are interesting. The goal is to convince them that *they* are interesting. Take all the energy you would usually spend trying to convince someone of what you are, and spend it trying to convince the other person of what *they* are. My students don't sit in my office because I talk to them; they sit in my office because I listen to them. If you want to make a friend, you need to start asking good questions.

In the 1936 classic *How to Win Friends and Influence People*, Dale Carnegie wrote, "Ask questions the other person will enjoy answering."[17]

In a Harvard study, researchers tasked participants to ask people a lot of questions during an online interaction.[18] Some were instructed to ask nine questions in fifteen minutes, and others were told to ask no more than four questions in fifteen minutes. What happened? People expressed the greatest amount of liking for people who asked them more questions. In fact, in a speed-dating experiment, asking just one more question on each speed date provided participants with an additional person at the end of the session who wanted to see them again.

So, first, if you want to be a better conversationalist, start asking questions. I would add, start mastering the follow-up question. Asking someone "how are you" is not going to necessarily let them know you are interested in knowing them. Say you are getting coffee and you bump into someone you know, a weak tie. You say, "How are you, Carol?" and Carol says, "I'm great!" And typically you mutter "great" back, and then you are dead in the water. Instead, insert a follow-up question.

Try, "Really? I'm happy to hear that. Has anything been especially great in particular?"

What you just did was send a signal to Carol that you aren't just saying hi to say hi. You care. You must care or you wouldn't have followed up.

Another easy question to ask as you are trying to strengthen a weak tie is simply to ask for advice. That is what Michael Jordan did when he contacted George Koehler. He asked where he should get his hair cut. You could invite people into a conversation by asking where they like to eat in the city. What's a great book they'd recommend? What is the last movie or show they watched that they loved? And then you follow up.

"What did you love about it?"

"How often do you go there?"

"Do you think it is something that I would enjoy?"

Some additional questions you could try are mirror questions. This is where you simply mirror what the other person has said. Carl asks, "What have you been up to?" and you respond, "Nothing much, what have you been up to?"

And if you are trying to take a relationship to a deeper level of intimacy—maybe going to dinner with a coworker to see if there is a potential friendship match or going on a second date with someone you have seen a movie with once before—you can try some questions that increase in depth.

"What do you like most about living here?"

"What place most feels like home to you?"

"What area of your work most excites you?"

Trying to go out and capture relational soul mates can be hard. Growth mates are easier to find. So look for people you can journey with. You are simply casting seeds and seeing which of them bear fruit. You don't have to convince someone you are funny. You don't have to trick them into believing you are more witty or exciting than you are. All you have to do is ask a few more questions. All you have to do is put yourself out there a bit more than you typically would. And if you get to know someone and decide you don't have much in common, there is no shame in moving them to your weak-tie group. You don't have to always go through this deep cognitive burden of mentally breaking up with people. You can just say, I am going to weaken this tie. Weak ties are still valuable. Your decision to remove someone from strong-tie status is not removing their humanity. All of our ties have value. It is okay to decrease the role someone plays in your life without feeling like you've decreased their dignity. All human beings, and all human relationships, whether strong ties or weak ones, make us better.

• • • •

It's time to write your seed list. If you were to throw yourself a party this year, what five people would you invite? This is where we are going to start, with these five names. We are going to be more intentional when we see them. We are going to ask them more questions. We are going to have follow-up questions ready. We are going to stop thinking we are looking for a soul mate and just start valuing our ties. We are going to change so we can truly live. Every day brings new opportunities. Every moment has possibility. None of us knows, hour by hour, what seed we plant that may actually grow. Faith is what happens when we start believing again in tomorrow.

Let's pray:

Lord, help me to be faithful with these few seeds. May you multiply the relationships you have put in my hand. Give me strength and confidence to try new things and make new invitations. And give me the time and patience to notice those whose invitations I have ignored. Here are my seeds, Lord. Have your way. Amen.

Seed List

1. _____

2. _____

3. _____

4. _____

5. _____

"Ask and it will be given to you; seek and you will find; knock and the door will be opened to you." (Matt. 7:7)

ENGAGE

- *Think about your closest friend. Tell the story of how you met.*

- *What are some good questions you could start adding to your casual conversations so you are ready when an opportunity presents itself?*
- *Who is a weak tie who has brought value to your life? Have you told them? How could you express your gratitude?*

CHAPTER 10

The Thing I'd Want
Before I Die

*Staying here, blaming them, and forever defining
your life by what they did will only increase the pain.
Worse, it will keep projecting out onto others. The
more our pain consumes us, the more it will control
us. And sadly, it's those who least deserve to be hurt
whom our unresolved pain will hurt the most.*

LYSA TERKEURST

Several years ago I (Seth) taught a monthly self-awareness class
at the Center for the Homeless in South Bend, Indiana. During
an activity in class I asked everyone to chronicle their major life
events so we could talk about them as a group. Before going to
the shelter, I didn't understand that many of the families and
individuals living there were in fact hardworking people who

just couldn't afford housing. Not everyone who is homeless is unemployed. I met people with full-time cashier jobs who were still unhoused. Homelessness is much more complicated than we think.

We had single mothers with several children who were trying to go back to school and were working full time at the nearby Walmart to make ends meet. Women who had left everything to flee domestic violence. I learned that sometimes drug and alcohol addiction have nothing to do with why some people end up at a shelter. For some, it's lack of family support when they need it the most. In the shelter are former professors and other working professionals who had a mental break due to hard circumstances and they simply fell apart. Deaths that left a once-functioning person totally incapacitated. If you have family support, you lean into their arms. If you don't, where do you lean?

Others had divorces that left them with nothing. Some fell into drugs and alcohol as a result of the life events mentioned above and bad coping strategies to deal with deep pain. My heart went out to them.

Shelters were answering the prayers of people who had nowhere else to go. This became their temporary haven of rest. The services provided at this place showed me a picture of the gospel more clearly than any sermon I've ever heard. Some of the workers were living out what it means to love your neighbor, not just talk about it. It moved me. It changed how I chose to do my own ministry. Communities need service.

On one of my visits we were in our two-hour teaching session when I asked the same question I always did.

"What is something you would want to do before you die?"

Some said, "Finish college."

Others said, "Own a home again."

And some said, "Go on a cruise."

I remember a gentleman I'll call Jim. He didn't give an answer. Jim was in his midseventies, and you could see he was contemplating whether or not he should share what was on his heart. The room fell silent as tears started to roll down his wrinkled skin. You knew by simply looking at Jim that his life was filled with a lot of hardship.

"Jim," I said, trying to provide him with an out, "you don't have to share if you don't want to."

"I'd want to be forgiven," he said with tears rolling down.

The whole room stilled. I wondered if his children knew. I wondered if his family or friends would be stunned to hear his deepest wish. I wondered if he'd ever get the only thing he truly wanted.

Forgiveness Is for You

Forgiveness goes far beyond our emotional ability to repair a relationship with someone who has wronged us. As Heather said in chapter 5, some relationships are not safe to continue after certain wrongs have been committed. A great resource for you if you need to go deeper into what forgiveness looks like, what healthy boundaries are, what is required of us as Christians is Lysa TerKeurst's book *Forgiving What You Can't Forget*.[1] *I'll See You Tomorrow* is about relational resilience, and I want to walk you through the positive aspects of forgiveness, because in a callout culture such as we have today, I believe we need more people willing to do the work of reconciliation. It's not popular, but forgiveness could give you your life back.

Karen Swartz, director of the Adult Mood Disorders Consultation Clinic at Johns Hopkins Hospital, noted, "Studies have found that the act of forgiveness can reap huge rewards for your health, lowering the risk of heart attack; improving cholesterol levels and sleep; and reducing pain, blood pressure, and levels of anxiety, depression and stress. And research points to an increase in the forgiveness-health connection as you age."[2]

The inner need to be forgiven is one of the strongest desires we can experience as people. It's like being set free. But to forgive someone of the pain they've caused you, to not carry the bitterness, the anger, the pain everywhere you go, there is freedom in that too. Releasing someone back to God, trusting the Lord to have the last word over our ache, that is freedom in Christ. Forgiving others actually makes us physically healthier. The reality is that although some people hurt us once, the burden that the experience forces us to carry lasts long after the original offense is over. Releasing people to God is not simply for them; it is for us. It is refusing to carry them any longer. It is the active process of taking the burden we never asked to carry and handing it to the God who has said he will. Forgiveness is taking back what someone else has taken. Forgiveness is healing. And it is worth our effort.

Forgiveness, according to Swartz, is more than an emotion; it's an "active process" where a person sets aside "negative feelings whether a person deserves it or not."[3]

Forgiveness is the release of the pent-up pain, and it benefits the person giving the forgiveness outside of whether the transgressor feels remorseful for their actions or if they ever accept the offered forgiveness. Forgiveness is about restoring us to our-selves. One of the things people can do, according to Swartz, is "seal it with an action," such as writing it down. If the pain was too great to address it to the person directly, or if it wouldn't be safe to sit down with that person because of the nature of their wrong action toward you, talking it out with someone else may be a good second option. Call a friend you trust. Schedule an appointment with your therapist. Healing may be on the other side of these conversations.

If it is safe to reengage with the other person, another way to seal it with an action is to pick up the phone. The week that COVID put the United States into lockdown was the same week the lead pastor at my church took a position at another congre-gation, and I went from being the youth pastor to interim lead pastor. This wasn't an ideal situation, and I was unsure of how to chart a successful path forward. I had earned the trust of the youth and young adults, but the larger congregation didn't really know me. They just saw me as the youth pastor, not as their leader.

That's when Heather and I decided to do something very simple, something we can all do when we are trying to either repair a relationship or form a deeper one. We picked up the phone to reach out to people. We printed the directory of every member's name that was on the books, whether they were regu-lar attenders or hadn't come to church in a while, and we called them. We called hundreds of people. Heather and I sat on oppo-site sides of our living room and called every single member on that list. We wanted to let them know that we were thinking about them during this confusing time, and we asked if there was anything they needed.

By dialing each member's number and saying, "Hello, this is Pastor Seth, and I just wanted to check in on you," I planted a seed. And this seed would take time and intentional effort to foster over the coming months if I wanted to see that relationship grow.

My suggestion to you, if you don't know where to start, is to call. If you don't know how to get the forgiveness you need, start by planting a seed. A call is the simplest thing we can do, but it often feels like the hardest. If they don't answer, leave a message telling them that you just wanted to check in and see how they were doing. I can't promise you I know what their reaction will be, but at least you've done what you could do when the ball was in your hands. At least you were faithful with your seed.

The Fetzer Institute found that 62 percent of Americans believe they need more forgiveness, but 58 percent believe there are instances when somebody should never be forgiven.[4] I am fascinated by these numbers because it feels so realistic to our lives. It shows in numerical form the duality that we each exist in as human beings. Everyone needs to be forgiven. And everyone has had something done to them that feels unforgivable. This may add a little clarity to what forgiveness means in Scripture and why Jesus often emphasized the need to offer forgiveness and to receive it.

Jesus said, "Therefore, I tell you, her many sins have been forgiven—as her great love has shown. But whoever has been forgiven little loves little" (Luke 7:47). The Lord says that once we have experienced forgiveness, we know its power, and we will try to set other people free. In other words, forgiving people could be exactly what creates more forgiveness. Sometimes the things we go through that we think disqualify us from connection, from worthiness, from peace are the same things that make us so sensitive to a world so void of it.

I notice the people others look past. I worked for years in junior high schools, and every school system I worked for served at-risk populations. I tend to run into spaces other people run away from because I know how much it matters to a twelve-year-old boy to have an adult male toss you a basketball. I don't feel uncomfortable in uncomfortable spaces, and that's because comfortability is less familiar to me. God has used the worst pieces of myself to reach into the worst pieces of someone else, and that is a purpose no one can take from me. Do I wish I was more outgoing? Yes. Do I wish I had a naturally more positive outlook? My wife would say, "God, please!" Do I wish sadness wasn't my most familiar emotion? Yes. But I have to forgive myself for who I am not so God can use me for who I am.

The Barna Group did a study on forgiveness and found that nine out of ten people who say they have received forgiveness say they then gave it in return. Speaking on Luke 7:47, Barna noted, "Jesus draws a connection between those who have been greatly forgiven and those who shown great love. Similarly, this study suggests that those who experience radical forgiveness have more willingness to forgive others."[5] The thing is that it takes forgiveness to make a world that gives it more freely.

Heather wrote in the last chapter, "You won't ever see the fruit while staring at the seed. Seeds feel so insignificant. They are tiny, easy to lose, and take a lot of energy to transform. But if you want a fruitful life, you are going to have to plant some seeds." Forgiveness is a seed. We don't just plant it to free ourselves; we plant it because it may free someone else. What if on the other side of our pain is purpose?

The prophet Hosea preached, "For I desire mercy, and not sacrifice; and the knowledge of God more than burnt offerings" (6:6 WEB). But mercy can't just be something we give someone else; it must be something we give ourselves. We must forgive ourselves for clutching our pain so tightly. Forgive ourselves for wasting so much time. Have mercy on ourselves for not knowing how to pick anything else up when our arms were already so full. Remember Luke 7:47? Those who experience forgiveness can also give it. Forgiveness, however, can't start with them. It has to start with you. We must forgive ourselves for all the anger we have buried. How can we give the light of mercy to others if all we feel ourselves is darkness?

Forgiveness Is for Them

There are people in my life who I think I've forgiven until something triggers the pain they've caused me, and my body remembers how hurt I still am. When I search my heart, I have to pull out the skeletons, the ones that very few people know about. When I have to ask God to help me to forgive, it is like I'm handing Christ all my bones. They look much scarier when they are in the dark. Why was I cradling them?

Maybe it is time for you to do the same. Open the door and let some light in. Set the skeletons down, acknowledge how heavy they've been. In the book *Compassion (&) Conviction*, Justin Giboney, Michael Wear, and Chris Butler revealed a powerful truth to me: "Love is about willing the good for another."[6] To truly love one another is not just about forgiving them; it is about willing that they would change. What does justice look like?

What does healing look like? What does restoration look like? What if it looks like willing the good for the other?

I can tell you that at moments in my life I haven't always willed the good for the other. I've willed vengeance. I've prayed for judgment. They made their bed, so let them cry in it. How can I will the good for people who are so clearly bad? The truth is, harbored resentment has hurt me more than the initial event itself. For years I have lost sleep, sat in anger, lived in silent agony, and clutched my bones. And then I wonder why it is so hard for me to make friends. I am not even sure if I couldn't let go of my pain or if I didn't want to. If you hold something close enough and long enough, it will feel more and more valuable. It is also very hard to pick up something when you are already tightly squeezing something else. Even when I met Heather, I wanted to hold on to her, but my heart already felt so full of things I truly didn't want. There was something scary about that. I was opening myself up to the possibility of more hurt. People who don't understand that relationships are scary probably don't have as many bones in their basement.

I have a sermon illustration in which I tell someone onstage to hold out a wallet. "The wallet," I say, "symbolizes your finances." Then I ask them to hold out their keys. "Your keys," I say, "symbolize possessions." Then I have them take some books to symbolize their studies and education. I hand them a photo to symbolize their family. A ring to symbolize their romantic pursuits.

"And this," I say, "is God." I pull out a basketball and hold it up for everyone to see. "I want you to follow and pursue the Lord with all your heart, with all your strength, and with all your might." And I ask if they are ready for me to toss them the basketball. The problem is, their hands are already holding so many other objects. They are already holding on to so much stuff. It looks impossible to hold on to God when your hands are already full. The only way to do it is to put the other stuff down and pick up God. Then, if you focus, if you are intentional, you can put the other stuff in your hands, but only if God (the basketball) is what you hold first. There may be stuff you have to put down, but you can't even make those choices until first things come first.

That is what we do with forgiveness. It feels impossible to pick it up if you are already holding on to all of your other stuff. How can I forgive a church member when I am so angry at them? How can you forgive your husband when you are rightfully so bitter? How do we forgive our parents or our coworkers or our friends when we are holding on to all the painful stuff that reminds us of what they did? What if we can't? What if we have to put it down first? And it's not that we can't pick it back up. It's not that we can't be honest that wounds have been made. It's that we have to hold forgiveness first. It's that we have to will the good for the other. God will do all the rearranging of what else we can carry. The truth is, until we set some things down, we don't know how much more our hands are capable of holding. What if joy is still available to sit beside your pain? What if it is possible for the family you create to sit beside the family you never had? What if it is possible for the dreams you'll still accomplish to rest beside the ones you lost? I didn't grow up holding my father's hand, but my kids will grow up able to hold mine. That's what God's justice looks like. Forgiveness creates more forgiveness. Trust builds more trust. If we want to let go of some of our darkness, we have to let in the light.

Jim may never be forgiven by his kids. He may never get to show them that he takes ownership of his actions. He may never reconcile with a family he left behind. Sometimes we will wait for an apology that never comes. You can't control what other people do with the things that are in their hands. All you can do is decide what you want to place in yours. So what is the one thing you would want to do before you die? I hope your answer is to pick up whatever lets you most fully live.

• • • •

Jesus said, "Father, forgive them, for they do not know what they are doing." (Luke 23:34)

ENGAGE

- *How does the word* forgiveness *make you feel? Why?*
- *Is it possible to offer someone forgiveness who hasn't asked for it and may never apologize?*
- *Who forgave you? What was that experience like?*

CHAPTER 11

Chaos or Community

A social movement that only moves people is merely a revolt. A movement that changes both people and institutions is a revolution.

MARTIN LUTHER KING JR.

Ellen DeGeneres: canceled. Vanessa Hudgens: canceled. J. K. Rowling: canceled. These are just a few of the people who were canceled in 2020. In that year we learned that cancel culture is when we cancel brands, shows, or movies that we find to be problematic.[1] Just ask Roseanne Barr.

For the purposes of this conversation, I (Heather) am defining cancel culture as the steamrolling of a public figure, brand, or product because of a perceived public error. Seth just shared with you a truly beautiful, poetic story of forgiveness. But let's be honest, it feels oh-so-good to give people what they deserve.

I am not going to tell you there isn't a place for handing people the wage they earned; there certainly is. It is important for people within a society to make decisions about the thought leaders we believe deserve to have a platform. In fact, I think it is healthy to de-platform people for continued bad behavior. But should we treat everyday people like industry leaders? Should we cancel our grandmother because of the person she votes for? Should we cancel our friends for watching the wrong news station? If we value humanity, shouldn't we try to see the person behind the perceived poison? Already someone's fingers are burning to log on to Twitter and cancel me, Seth, and this book, but you may be exactly the type of person who needs to read this. Slow down, Brad.

My concern is that we are raising a generation of people who cancel others as soon as they do one thing they disagree with. I am all for accountability, but this is dangerous. Primarily because human beings are imperfect people. The entire point of the gospel is that people generally suck, which is why we need a Savior. Seth hit the nail on the head. We are all, sinner and saint, in need of grace and forgiveness. Christianity is not a flattering religion. You don't become a Christian because you are great; you become a Christian because you realize you aren't that great and need some help. Grace, redemption, growth. All of these are a deep part of the Christian experience. Accountability is important, but I hope we leave room for people to change. The Heather of today would absolutely have canceled the Heather of four years ago. I am constantly in awe of how gentle God has been with me. Do we want people to be canceled or do we want people to change? One leads to chaos. One leads to community.

It is so much easier to cancel people online. I remember life before this, but Generation Z members don't. They've grown up in the era of the cancel. My childhood was characterized by *Barney & Friends* and *Full House*. I was raised to talk things through and look for common ground. I am one after-school special away from asking if you want to hug me after a "crucial conversation." But we are living in a day where it seems the bigger person is the weaker one. Does the phrase "Twitter do your thing" mean anything to you? Twitter is where Jerry Springer went after they canceled his talk show. Facebook is savage. I am fine with hot girls posting photos of themselves with a Bible verse if it means no one is yelling at me on Instagram. (I will hold your ring light, Rachel.) But as we are posting, may we never forget our entire religion hinges on loving thy neighbor as thyself. The good Samaritan is our mantra, and yet most of us would have taken a video of the beaten man on the Jericho road if it meant we would get viral views.

Twitter has changed our generation in ways no other social platform has. Perhaps because the average user has far fewer followers than their Facebook networks, it kind of feels like you are just tossing paper confetti into a windstorm. Every ounce of shade you wish you could throw in person is like a grenade in your hands on Twitter. Online, you don't have to be the bigger person. In fact, you are rewarded for your bite. Mouthing off to your boss is risky, but sharing a meme directed at him on social media is vague and easy. The reach of Twitter was really proven in 2013 when Justine Sacco was famously fired from her job within hours of sending a comment into the abyss that is cyberspace.[2] This is a fact: it took eleven hours.

She tweeted, "Going to Africa. Hope I don't get AIDS. Just kidding. I'm white!"

And she was unemployed before her plane even landed. Her tweet went viral and a hashtag (#hasJustinelandedyet) was trending on BuzzFeed before she finished her in-flight pretzels. I don't know where Justine is now, but more than I want her canceled, I want her to change. I want her to realize the power of her ignorance. I want her to know the power of words. And I want you to realize the power of yours. Social media exaggerates who we are in real life.

Seth once tweeted, "After I tweet, I just stare at my phone until someone likes it." And I snorted after hitting Like, because it was true. We will say anything, no matter how visceral, if we think it will get us hits. It's as if we no longer register the fact that our words hold power and have a huge impact on people. It's a meat fest and everyone's a carnivore. I've seen childhood friends I've always known to be shy and soft-spoken dunk like LeBron James on an account with two followers, and it feels as if I don't know who anyone is anymore. Every profile picture is a person. (Well, most of them. Some are bots engineered to spiral you into a perpetual rage, but that is a point for another day.)

I just read in the book of James that "mercy triumphs over judgment" (2:13), but clearly not online and clearly not in church. Our nation is in a crisis, and nothing really displays it more than our news feeds. It's a 24/7 roid rage, and I am honestly embarrassed for my kids to receive the world we are handing them. It's Democrats versus Republicans, vegans versus the meat industry, and Elon Musk versus everyone else. We love touting mercy when it is extended to people we think deserve it. But the Bible says we should be "quick to listen, slow to speak and slow to become angry" (James 1:19). Instead, we are quick to tweet, slow to listen, and ready to block you and your mom if you want to @ me.

Remember that communication theory says we can't control the message of another. If we want to stop a cycle, we must control our reaction to it. I can't change your response, but I can change mine. At some point, as Christians, the forgiven becomes the forgiver. Canceling may be necessary, but it shouldn't be our initial reaction to every issue in a relationship. Again, it comes back to chapter 1 and the fact that we typically can't decide who someone is based on isolated incidents. We must look at who someone has shown us they are over the span of our entire relationship. Grace has always been for people who don't deserve it. What does winning look like?

Where Do We Go from Here?

In the August heat of 1965, widespread violence and bloodshed tore through the Watts area of Los Angeles. There were more than thirty deaths. Most of those were perpetrated by the police. There was fire and looting and vandalism. At the invitation of black social groups, civil rights leader Martin Luther King Jr. entered Watts. He later described the protests that followed as "disorganized," though that was a major oversimplification. "However, a mere condemnation of violence is empty without understanding the daily violence that our society inflicts upon many of its members," he said. "The violence of poverty and humiliation hurts as intensely as the violence of the club."[3]

King wrote about his interaction with a couple of young men

in the wake of the weeklong eruption that destroyed many black businesses that had been the heart of the community.

"We won!" King remembers hearing one exclaim.[4]

He looked at the rubble. The ash. The broken buildings. He tallied the dead bodies.

"What does winning look like?" he asked the youth.

It is against this backdrop of the voting victories of the civil rights movement, along with the ache and burden of the worsening condition for many black communities, that King wrote *Where Do We Go from Here?*[5] It is an expansion of the conversation that began during his 1965 March on Selma, where he famously and boldly said, "We must keep going."[6]

The devastation people are experiencing today is like a wall so high none of us can see the sunlight anymore. Businesses are crumbling. Churches are dividing. A pandemic is raging. Police brutality is still present. In fact, George Floyd was surely just one of a thousand police killings in 2020.

I am not being facetious when I say that. There were 996 fatal police shootings in 2018 and 1004 in 2019, with African Americans being more likely than any other ethnicity to be killed by police.[7] It feels as though the weight of sin has slowly sucked all the oxygen out from the planet and we are all slowly suffocating beneath it.

"What does winning look like?" King and those with him asked the youth in Watts. And it is a question we must also ask ourselves today.

King wrote *Where Do We Go from Here?* in Jamaica. He rented a secluded house that had no telephone so he could labor with love and attention over the manuscript that would be the culmination of a decade-long fight for justice. This was one of

King's few experiences with solitude. He was the man behind a movement that had changed and would continue to change the course of American history. At the time of King's death in 1968, he had a disapproval rating of 75 percent.[8] The man we now revere, the man whose achievements we spend an entire day acknowledging, is the man who was both imprisoned and murdered. "Where do we go from here?" I think King would still ask us. "Chaos or community?"

A World in Chaos

Today, America as a country is at war with itself. And we aren't just at war with people of other races and we aren't just at war with Christianity; our divide seems to be a tribalism so strong that it is separating people of the same family and origin. In fact, a Stanford study found that Americans' strongest attachment, more than their religion, more than their race, more than the language they speak, is to their political party.[9] We are a country divided and a country in chaos.

In the book *Invisible Influence*, Jonah Berger explains the driving force of the attitude and opinions we vote on. One would think the decisions we make in the voting booth are made because we hold deeply personal convictions about how our country should be run, how much aid is too much aid, and what constitutes a government overreach. Some of us are just naturally liberal and others are naturally conservative, right? Of course we see things differently and stand behind our convictions. That is what I thought too. Until I read *Invisible Influence*. In it, Berger relays the findings of a Yale study titled

"Party Over Policy: The Dominating Impact of Group Influence on Political Beliefs."

In the study, participants were randomly assigned to read one of two versions of a welfare policy report in a fictional newspaper that they did not know was fictional. One was termed the "generous policy" and one was the "stringent policy."[10] The differences between the two policies were the amount of government aid provided to recipients. Berger observed, "When we think about attitudes toward social policies like these, we usually think they are driven by our own personal opinions. Our own beliefs about our feelings toward the issues . . . so it wouldn't be surprising if conservatives preferred more stringent welfare policies while liberals preferred more generous ones."[11]

And that is exactly what happened. Conservatives loved the stringent welfare policy, and liberals thought it was terrible. But the study didn't care about the policies; it wanted to look at the impact of group influence on our beliefs. Remember Social Judgment Theory? Our judgments are decisions we make based on social networks. So the researchers told the people who read the generous policy that it was supported by 95 percent of Republicans. You'd think Republicans would hate a generous welfare policy offering massive aid and education benefits to poor people. But guess what? They didn't. When Republicans were told that other Republicans liked the policy, their position on the policy changed. In fact, they loved it. They now loved what they once hated. And the only reason was because of who else loved it.

At this point liberals are nodding their heads. *Of course Republicans don't think for themselves*, they chuckle. But liberals were just as likely as Republicans to change their position when they found out that the stringent bill (which liberals would traditionally hate) was favored by 95 percent of Democrats. That is what happens to social creatures such as human beings when we are a part of a group. We tend to mirror them. We change even our personal beliefs to better fit within our group. We make social judgments. That is what Berger called *invisible influence*, and it is happening all around us. We decide what we believe based on who else believes it. And we decide what we should hate based on who our groups deem the enemy. The groups we are a part of can challenge us toward greater empathy, a deeper value of humanity, and a greater pursuit of the gospel. Or they can lead us toward more division, disruption, and disunity. Even in an individualistic country, such as the United States, our groups create an invisible influence.

So we are living in a country where Americans feel their political affiliation is their greatest form of identity attachment, more than their race or religion, and yet how that political affiliation plays out in their real-life thoughts, attitudes, opinions, and beliefs is not at all a solitary decision. Our groups are shaping us. For better or for worse, the social group you identify with will make you look more like Jesus or less like Jesus. And one day we will all have to stand before Jesus and be accountable for how we lived here. Did we sow community? Did we create chaos? Did we will the good for the other?

The groups you identify with are not just reinforcing things you already believe; they can also radicalize beliefs you never had. Our social ties, both weak and strong ones, make up how we navigate our social worlds. And some of us are drowning because the people on our ship have told us we are better off if we sink. Some of us are hopeless because the people in our circles have told us that hope is dead. Some of us are sitting in fire and ash because the groups with which we identify have told us that we must let hope burn. But what if who we are today isn't who we were meant to be? And what if the gospel can truly breathe new life into a world dying from strangulation? It has never been more important to ask ourselves what winning looks like.

Community

In the gospel, winning looks like community. It looks like the individual looking out for the whole. It looks like a decision to love God and love the people around us. It looks like the reunification of the family of believers. It looks like a family of God bringing heaven to earth. I want you to put down your predetermined labels for a moment. I want you to lay aside your race, your political affiliation, and even your religion for a moment. And I want to tell you about Jesus. The teachings of Jesus are widely accepted to be beautiful wisdom on the value of love and human belonging. The long-shared quote by Mohandas Gandhi is "I like your Christ. I do not like your Christians. Your Christians are so unlike your Christ."[12]

Scripture says, "They are from the world and therefore speak from the viewpoint of the world, and the world listens to them" (1 John 4:5). This single verse almost answers the question Martin Luther King Jr. must have asked himself implicitly before writing his book. "Where are we from?" is typically asked before "Where do we go from here?"

I believe, especially after reading King's speech "Beyond Vietnam: A Time to Break Silence," that he would point us as a nation to 1 John 4:7–8: "Dear friends, let us love one another, for love comes from God. Everyone who loves has been born of God and knows God. Whoever does not love does not know God, because God is love."

In his speech, King said, "This call for a worldwide fellowship that lifts neighborly concern beyond one's tribe, race, class, and nation is in reality a call for an all-embracing—embracing and unconditional love for all mankind. This oft misunderstood, this oft misinterpreted concept, so readily dismissed by the Nietzsches of the world as a weak and cowardly force, has now become an absolute necessity for the survival of man."[13]

Does any of this sound familiar to you? Even within the tribe of Christianity I am reading think pieces by professed Christians against empathy. The idea that love is somehow a weak power is an insult to the Christ who came lowly, riding on a donkey to proclaim it.

King continued:

When I speak of love I am not speaking of some sentimental and weak response. I am not speaking of that force which is just emotional bosh. I am speaking of that force which all of the great religions have seen as the supreme unifying principle of life. Love is somehow the key that unlocks the door which leads to ultimate reality. This Hindu-Muslim-Christian-Jewish-Buddhist belief about ultimate—ultimate reality is beautifully summed up in the first epistle of Saint John: "Let us love one another; for love is of God. And every one that loveth is born of God and knoweth God. He that loveth not knoweth not God, for God is love." "If we love one another, God dwelleth in us, and his love is perfected in us."[14]

The devil would love to see the world sink into chaos. The spirits of darkness would love to see the divisions that have arisen deplete us, not from outside but from within. I can't shake the image Seth provided us from the shelter that day, a man who just wanted to know that he is forgiven. The spirit of unforgiveness holds us hostage more than our enemies. The burden of hate will cause our arms to grow so heavy. And none of this is new. Every sinking feeling of hopelessness, the world has felt before. Every crushing weight of anxiety and depression and division has been felt before. The question "where do we go from here" has been asked before. Toward chaos? Toward community? But know, before you choose, that the groups you identify with may deeply influence how you see the problems we face. Which is why I ask you to lay them down for just a few more moments. You can pick them all back up again, but not until you've picked up your cross.

The symbol of the Christian is not Fox News or CNN. It is certainly not a nation's flag. It is not Republican or Democrat, and it is not party lines. The symbol of the Christian is the cross. It is to pick up the burden of our fellow human beings and walk toward the dusty, long road that leads us to the redemptive work that is found within the kingdom of God. It is a cross that belongs to all nations. It is a cross that has no dominant language. It is a cross that does not belong to a country or a political party or a denomination. The cross belongs to the King of the world on whom all authority has been given on both heaven and earth (Matt. 28:18). The cross belongs to Christ. And Christ is the unifier of us all.

Pastor David Asscherick preached a sermon titled "Gospel Tribe," where he relays Revelation 7 beautifully. In Revelation 7:9, when John saw heaven, he saw a multitude that no one could number: "After this I looked, and there before me was a great multitude that no one could count, from every nation, tribe, people and language, standing before the throne and before the Lamb."

Heaven is not a place for the few. Heaven will not belong to a single tribe. John saw in a vision an innumerable multitude. They did not share a common language. They did not all share the same denomination. They certainly were not all the same political affiliation. Do you want to know what they all had in common? We see that in verse 10: "They cried out in a loud voice: 'Salvation belongs to our God.'" So we have people of different countries with different languages and races and beliefs and ideologies, who undoubtedly differ on a variety of issues, and yet they are similar only in the fact that they all cry out in unison that he is "our" God.

In Selma in 1965 Martin Luther King Jr. said, "We must keep going." And we, too, must keep walking toward tomorrow. In 1967 King said, "Let us hope that this spirit will become the order of the day. We can no longer afford to worship the god of hate or bow before the altar of retaliation. The oceans of history are made turbulent by the ever-rising tides of hate. And history is cluttered with the wreckage of nations and individuals that pursued this self-defeating path of hate."[15]

Our lives are still cluttered and our churches are still cluttered and our movements are still cluttered with individuals who pursue this self-defeating path of hate. You may pick up all of your identities now. All the things that make us who we are matter; they make a difference. All the things that impact our experiences only help us better connect to one another. For Christians, however, they should always be placed beneath the cross. The symbol of our walk is not who we are but who we become in Christ. The transformative work of the gospel is that it makes us new. He takes our hearts of stone and gives us hearts of flesh (Ezek. 36:26).

So where do we go from here? What does winning look like? Do we choose chaos or community? We must all answer these questions for ourselves.

I leave you with some more words from Martin Luther King Jr. Read them and feel the urgency within them. King was a man who actually gave his life to defend the brotherhood and sisterhood of humanity he believed was still possible.

> We are now faced with the fact, my friends, that tomorrow is today. We are confronted with the fierce urgency of now. In this unfolding conundrum of life and history, there is such a thing as being too late. Procrastination is still the thief of time. Life often leaves us standing bare, naked, and dejected with a lost opportunity.[16]

This may well be our last chance to choose between chaos or community. I suppose that is the one drawback of always saying, "I'll see you tomorrow." Sometimes waiting for tomorrow delays what must truly be done today.

• • • •

> If anyone says, "I love God," and hates his brother, he is a liar; for he who does not love his brother whom he has seen cannot love God whom he has not seen. (1 John 4:20 ESV)

ENGAGE

- *What does winning in your life look like?*
- *What does it mean to choose community over division?*
- *Where do we go from here? How do we change the climate of hate? As a church? As a nation? Personally?*

CHAPTER 12

Old Foundation,
New House

*Nobody remembers if you cross the finish line bruised
and bloody. They just remember that you stayed the
course. Don't get hung up on how ugly the race may
have looked. In the end, all that matters is that you
finish.*

CHIP GAINES

Several years ago I (Seth) was sitting in the office of Duane
Covrig, one of my professors at Andrews University. He taught
in the leadership department, and he was giving me counsel on
my life. Mapping out all the different events, both good and bad,
he said, "Seth, your life right now looks like a crooked path."

Grabbing a pen and paper he drew random dots for each life

event I had experienced. Very slowly he connected each dot until they were all joined together.

He said, "I think this is what Isaiah 45:2 means when it reads, 'I will go before thee, and make the crooked places straight.'"

Life is about dots. One here, one there, and it feels as we move from point to point that there is no purpose to the madness. That is, not until we reach our destination. Only after we get to our ending point do we realize the dots connected all along. That God truly does make crooked paths straight.

Together, we have journeyed from dot to dot. We learned about stress and how it impacts our bodies and that relationships are the antidote. We learned that waiting for the ideal can prevent us from doing what is still possible. We learned that life is about finding a pace we can sustain. We discovered that *no* is not a bad word and that some relationships must be dumped. The dots of our time together remind us that new experiences are the only way to get out of old cages. The next time your brain shuts down and you feel yourself freeze, I want you to hear Heather's voice whisper, "It's okay. Your brain is just trying to protect you." As you move on and life brings you new dots, I hope you will remember that change won't be easy, but it will be necessary. I hope you will forgive yourself for any time you may have wasted. And I hope you will choose community over chaos.

The thing about life is it doesn't make much sense as we walk through it day by day, little by little, dot by dot. And while the journey toward hope won't be linear, I want you to know that it is no mistake that you are who you are. God will make your crooked path straight. God will connect your dots.

What Is Possible from Your Old Foundation

I told you earlier that Heather and I had put in offers on five houses before we finally bought one. It is a California ranch that was originally built in 1960. It had one owner. He was a former CBS executive who took a job in Michigan to do marketing for a hospital. When his family came here, they brought the blueprints for their home in California, which they had loved. A five-bedroom, three-bath, spacious ranch with cathedral ceilings. In its day, this house was probably the talk of the block. But sixty years had passed. Trends came and went. Colors went out of style. Stains from children who grew into teenagers left their memories on the carpet. When our Realtor, Dave Jardine, showed us the house, he said, "Heather, the second I saw this home, I knew you would love it." He had shown us dozens of houses at this point. He had helped us make offers on four of them. He knew my wife's taste, and he was right. Heather's eyes lit up. The biggest thing Heather looks for in a home is space, ceilings, and character. She doesn't like the cookie-cutter new constructions. She likes an old foundation that we can renovate into a new house—and by "we" she means me.

We immediately made an offer. This was our house. We felt it. We could see it. We didn't care anymore that the other four houses had fallen through. This California ranch was worth waiting for. However, when we brought her family over, my mother-in-law didn't see what we saw. Where we saw character, she saw old. Where we saw potential, she saw work. She could not understand for the life of her why we would want to purchase a home that was going to cost us so much money to get into. And she told us she did not understand it—regularly. But we didn't care. We could see it.

Well, ten minutes into my renovation process, I found water under the carpet. The entire back door in the four-seasons room was rotted. The inspector didn't even catch it. It's fine. No big deal. Small setback. Next, the furnace went out. Then, when I tried to remove a weird platform in the floor of the dining room, which I am sure was a showstopper in the seventies, I found plumbing when I was halfway through removing the floor-boards. I panicked. I've done carpentry and house renovation work since high school. This is probably the only area of my life I am almost confident in. I may have failed my freshmen year of college, but Lord knows I can swing a hammer. But this house had more work beneath the floor than I had money to fix. I tried calling for reinforcements. I called some of my old painter friends from my construction days. But apparently things have changed since 2012. Inflation was high, and I realized I would have made more money in one week as a painter than I could in two months as a pastor.

So what do you do when life gives you more than you think you have the resources to complete? You do the work one day at a time, and that is exactly what I did and am still doing. I cut into walls and opened the area between the four-seasons room and the living room. I tore down the ceiling overhang that made the dining room feel smaller. Instead of lowering the floor, which was my original plan, I leveled all the other floors so they would be flush. I primed and I painted. I went to the hardware store more times than I can remember. I did the work. And it paid off.

Tonight, my mother-in-law stopped over. I could see the look of surprise cross her face. The house with the old foundation, the one that would be too much work to finish, the one that wasn't worth the effort, was beautiful. I watched her walk around the rooms and tell us where it would be a good idea to put a painting. She ate Thai food by my fireplace, and I could have imagined it, but I swear it looked as if she didn't want to leave. She finally saw what I knew was possible the entire time. She even pointed to one room and said, "This is where you should put the Christmas tree."

This house with the old foundation is where my family will make new memories. The floors that I had to level will be where my kids throw dance parties. And if you were to walk into my house next year, you would think it always looked this way. That is what happens when we build new houses on old foundations. People don't see the work; they see the win. Sometimes in life you have to see what is possible to believe the promise. Right now, on my wall, Heather and I hung a sign. If you ever come over, you will see it right when you enter the front door. It says "Old Foundation, New House." And it is not just symbolic of what I knew this house could be. It is symbolic of what I want to always remember God is doing in me. Growth is possible even on your old foundation.

Building Your New House

Psychologist Adam Grant said, "More than half the people who experience a traumatic event report at least one positive change, compared to less than 15 percent who develop PTSD."[1] More people experience growth after trauma than PTSD.

That doesn't mean it won't be work. That doesn't mean you

won't lift a floorboard and want to get the heck out of there. It doesn't mean you won't think you will run out of resources before any real progress can be seen. But I need you to know what I wish someone had told me. That there is a thing called post-traumatic growth. And seeing is believing.

Sheryl Sandberg and Adam Grant wrote in their book *Option B*, "Many find meaning in discovering religion or embracing spirituality. Traumatic experiences can lead to deeper faith, and people with strong religious and spiritual beliefs show greater resilience, and greater levels, of post-traumatic growth."[2]

I need you to know that deeper faith is available to you. I need you to know that it may just be your faith that has kept you connecting the dots this entire time. God will make your crooked path straight. You don't have to stay where you were. Growth is possible. In fact, it is more likely to be a product of your trauma than PTSD is.[3]

When I began this book, in the introduction, I told you that every Seth needs a Heather. Everyone deserves to have at least one cheerleader. Don't waste another moment waiting for what you thought should have been ideal for you to go and create what is still possible. If you don't have a friend, be a friend. If you don't have a mentor, be a mentor. If you don't have a safe place, create one for someone else.

Sandberg wrote, "It's not surprising that so many trauma survivors end up helping others overcome the adversity that they faced themselves. There is nothing more satisfying than helping someone else escape your same despair. . . . After going through hardship people have new knowledge to offer those who go through similar experiences. It's a unique source of meaning because it doesn't just give our lives purpose, it gives our suffering purpose. People help where they've been hurt and then wounds are not in vain."[14]

Your wounds are not in vain. There is a purpose to your life. So don't overlook the character forged in your foundation. Will the good for the other. In a world that's not ideal, go and do what is possible.

• • • •

Everyone then who hears these words of mine and does them will be like a wise man who built his house on the rock. And the rain fell, and the floods came, and the winds blew and beat on that house, but it did not fall, because it had been founded on the rock. (Matt. 7:24–25 esv)

ENGAGE

- What area of your life can you first start to rebuild?
- What negative experience has caused growth in your life?
- Who can you tell about the principles in I'll See You Tomorrow?

Conclusion

Dear Reader,

I (Heather) didn't walk for my master's graduation. I had been in school for six years at that point. Six years is a long time to work toward something. There are 312 weeks in six years. There are 2,190 days in six years. There are 52,560 hours in six years. Six years is not insignificant. And yet I didn't walk for my MA graduation.

I finished my BA in three and a half years. I did about twenty-three credit hours a semester and double majored. I didn't take a summer off. I had friends who went to Spain to make sure they'd be fluent in Spanish. I loved Spanish and spoke well enough conversationally, but there was no way I was taking a year off my graduation date to study abroad. When other people were hanging out with friends, I was writing papers. When people asked me to move into the dorms, I told them I didn't think that was a good idea. I stayed with my parents. Mainly because I wanted to make sure I stayed on track. I didn't view school as a social activity.

I tell my students now not to be the student that I was. I want so much more for them than that. I tell them to study abroad. Seth did. He served in Chuuk, Micronesia, for a year, and he will tell you that it was one of the most profoundly impactful years of his life.

It turns out no one cares if you graduated in three and a half years, but people will ask what you were doing in Portugal. No one will notice that you did twenty-three credit hours a semester, but people will be interested in what you learned about teamwork on the soccer pitch.

I was always so focused on where I was headed that I missed the people I was with. I think, in a lot of ways, for years I still did that. I was only as present in my job as I was with my next task. I don't want you to become what I was. I don't want you to be so focused on your project that you forget to tuck in your kids. I don't want you to be so engrossed in the email that you forget to ask if anyone wants to go with you to lunch.

Life is not about destinations. It is about traveling companions. Bermuda is beautiful. But sunsets are prettier when you have people to share them with. I want that for you.

Of the 46 percent of people who said they met three to six influential friends or mentors during college, 86 percent of them said they stayed in touch with that person after graduation.[1] Only 15 percent of people say they have real friends at work.[2] Americans spend on average 34.4 hours per week with people they are making no meaningful relationships with.[3] I think we are all so focused on where we are headed that we overlook the people we are with. I wish I had spent more time yesterday paying attention to what was in my hand. I wish I had lived in the moments that I was in. I wish I had savored every single dot.

Life doesn't give us do-overs. Yesterday doesn't let us walk through the moments again. Life doesn't let us try it on and decide how much we want to invest before living it. The problem with always looking at tomorrow is it causes you to miss today. Don't let fear of what could or could not happen cause you to miss the beauty of what is.

Michael Jordan said, "I've missed more than 9,000 shots in my career. I've lost almost 300 games. Twenty-six times I've been trusted to take the game-winning shot and missed. I've failed over and over and over again in my life. And that is why I succeed."[4] He succeeded because he engaged.

Clearly winning doesn't make us winners. There are people who have won who don't feel like champions. And losing doesn't make us failures. Michael Jordan has lost three hundred games. But committing to showing up does make us players, and what if what we are all playing is an infinite game? Michael Jordan isn't known as the greatest winner of all time; he is known as the greatest *player* of all time. Yet he missed nine thousand shots.

Don't let fear of what could or could not happen cause you to miss the beauty of what is. There is purpose for you right here. Your life doesn't start when you get to where you are going. Your life matters even in the middle. What is in your hand? What shots do you still need to take? What seeds has God called you to plant? There are people praying right now that you won't rush through your middle.

I graduated during December and went straight into my master's degree. No breaks. No celebratory march. I just registered for the next set of classes. I knew I wanted to teach. And to teach university students, I would need a PhD. I started planning my PhD program before I was done with my bachelor's degree.

I am what you would call a future-oriented person. I think about the future a lot. I get upset over things that haven't yet happened. The first thing I do if someone calls me about a possible job opportunity is look up the houses for sale in that area. I haven't even interviewed. But that's how my brain works. I plan for what's next. The present has always been an inconvenient block between me and what is surely on the way.

That's how I saw my master's degree: an inconvenient step between me and a PhD. It was a necessary middle point.

Seth is so much better at this than I am. He is so much better at embracing the present. I love that about him. He's taught me to see what is right in front of me.

My mother begged me to walk. She wanted to see me march. My parents were incredibly proud that I had finished a graduate program. Neither of them had that opportunity. I couldn't understand why my mother was so insistent that I purchase a gown and take a few pictures. It didn't make sense to me. I told her she could watch me walk once they conferred my PhD.

"What if you don't finish a PhD?" she asked. It was a fair question, but I was insulted at the suggestion.

"We will celebrate when I actually finish," I told her. This was my middle. This was a halfway point. My eyes were focused on tomorrow.

All around us, people are just barely hanging on. Which is why I want what we talk about today to strengthen your hands. I want to strengthen your hands because you have been called to strengthen someone else's. I know that about you, even if you don't know that about yourself.

What I want you to know about me is that I didn't walk for my MA graduation. I didn't allow myself to experience the beauty of today. What I want for you is what I wish I had done for me; I want you to celebrate your middles. Pay attention to your halfway points. Maybe you didn't get the job, but you should acknowledge that you completed the application. Maybe they didn't answer, but you should celebrate that you picked up the phone. I want you to be a better student of life than I have been. I want you to pay attention to growth and let yourself feel the joy that you are still engaging in the process. Play the game. Keep showing up. Take shots and miss them. Take a moment on the bench. But whatever you do, don't give up.

Maybe you aren't a totally transformed person today. But maybe you are better than you were yesterday. Doesn't that matter? Maybe you aren't free of your addiction. But maybe you were able to exit the web page you knew you shouldn't have opened. Shouldn't you take a moment and acknowledge that? Beginnings are beautiful, and endings make for some really great stories, but life is lived in the middle. Seth and I don't want you to miss that. Celebrate your middle. Celebrate the small steps throughout this journey. Be present with where you are and who is with you. What happens in your future depends on how you lived today. And one day, when we are in heaven, I hope you'll pull Seth and me aside. I hope you'll tell us about all the shots you missed. And about all the shots you made. Humanity is connected. Heaven is a small town. Strong ties and weak ones—each of us matters.

Like it or not, on earth, this is our team. Each one of us is a neighbor. It has been an honor to serve alongside you. And if, for whatever reason, the stars don't align, and our paths don't cross today, please always promise that *I'll see you tomorrow.*

• • • •

There they crucified him, and with him two others—one on each side and Jesus in the middle. (John 19:18)

Notes

Introduction

1. Dictionary.com, s.v. "vulnerability," accessed March 16, 2022, https://www.dictionary.com/browse/vulnerability.

Chapter 1

1. Charles Wesley, "Let the World Their Virtue Boast," Hymnary .org, accessed March 16, 2022, https://hymnary.org/text/let_the _world_their_virtue_boast.

2. Saul McLeod, "Maslow's Hierarchy of Needs," Simply Psychology, updated December 29, 2020, https://www .simplypsychology.org/maslow.html.

3. "Science News: Meaningful Relationships Can Help You Thrive," Science Daily, August 29, 2014, https://www .sciencedaily.com/releases/2014/08/140829084247.htm.

4. "How to Calm an Anxious Stomach: The Brain-Gut Connection," Anxiety and Depression Association of America, July 19, 2018, https://adaa.org/learn-from-us/from-the-experts /blog-posts/consumer/how-calm-anxious-stomach-brain -gut-connection.

5. Sara Reistad-Long, "6 of the Best Foods for an Upset Stomach," *Woman's Day*, August 30, 2016, https://www.womansday.com /health-fitness/nutrition/advice/g91/6-stomach-friendly-foods -105795/.

6. "Angelou," *Shambhala Sun*, January 1998, http://www.hartford
   -hwp.com/archives/45a/249.html.

7. *Oxford English Dictionary*, s.v. "peace," accessed March 16, 2022,
   https://www.oed.com/view/Entry/139215.

8. Allana Akhtar, "Michael Jordan on How to Handle High-Stress
   Pressure: 'Build Your Fundamentals,' Business Insider, June 2,
   2019, https://www.businessinsider.com/michael-jordan-reveals
   -how-to-handle-high-pressure-situations-2019-5.

9. Seth Franco, "Former Harlem Globetrotter: Seth Franco,"
   Westmore Church of God, August 24, 2015, YouTube video,
   35:32, https://www.youtube.com/watch?v=p2qc4pNY6XA.

10. Julia Cuttone, "Children Inspired by Former Harlem
    Globetrotter's Story," *Long Island Herald*, July 30, 2021, https://
    www.liherald.com/oysterbay/stories/children-inspired-by
    -former-harlem-globetrotters-story,133803.

Chapter 2

1. John McAloon, "Complex Trauma: How Abuse and Neglect
   Can Have Life-Long Effects," The Conversation, October 27,
   2014, https://theconversation.com/complex-trauma-how-abuse
   -and-neglect-can-have-life-long-effects-32329.

2. Jamie Marich, "How Is Trauma Different from Stress?" Gulf
   Bend Center, accessed February 19, 2022, https://www
   .gulfbend.org/poc/view_doc.php?type=doc&id=55726&cn
   =109 pg.1.

3. Kathryn Millán, "Trauma and Its Effect on Relationships,"
   Hartgrove Hospital, accessed February 19, 2022, https://www
   .hartgrovehospital.com/trauma-effect-relationships/.

4. Millan, "Trauma and Its Effect on Relationships."

5. Michelle Powers, "A Story in Every Stained Glass Window,"
   Currents News, April 30, 2014, YouTube video, 5:08, https://
   www.youtube.com/watch?v=8aXQE9q9BeE&t=73s.

6. The actual number of instances depends on which English
   translation you're using. "It came to pass" appears 452 times in

the King James Version (63 times in Genesis alone), 3 times in the English Standard Version, and not at all in the New American Standard Bible and the New International Version.

7. R. B. Brindley, "It Came to Pass," Bible Hub, accessed February 19, 2022, https://biblehub.com/sermons/auth/brindley/it_came_to_pass.htm.

8. See "Table FG10. Family Groups: 2020," US Census Bureau, "America's Families and Living Arrangements: 2020," Census.gov, updated October 8, 2021, https://www.census.gov/data/tables/2020/demo/families/cps-2020.html.

Chapter 3

1. Christopher McDougall, "Secrets of the Tarahumara," *Runner's World*, June 20, 2018, https://www.runnersworld.com/runners-stories/a20954821/born-to-run-secrets-of-the-tarahumara/.

2. McDougall, "Secrets of the Tarahumara."

3. McDougall, "Secrets of the Tarahumara."

4. Erica Turner and Lee Rainie, "Most Americans Rely on Their Own Research to Make Big Decisions, and That Often Means Online Searches," Pew Research Center, March 5, 2020, https://www.pewresearch.org/fact-tank/2020/03/05/most-americans-rely-on-their-own-research-to-make-big-decisions-and-that-often-means-online-searches/.

5. Stress in America 2021, "One Year Later, a New Wave of Pandemic Health Concerns," American Psychological Association, March 11, 2021, https://www.apa.org/news/press/releases/stress/2021/one-year-pandemic-stress.

6. Staying Healthy, "Why Stress Causes People to Overeat," *Harvard Health*, February 15, 2021, https://www.health.harvard.edu/staying-healthy/why-stress-causes-people-to-overeat.

7. Staying Healthy, "Why Stress Causes People to Overeat."

8. Health Essentials, "How Stress Can Make You Eat More—or Not at All," Cleveland Clinic, July 1, 2020, https://health.clevelandclinic.org/how-stress-can-make-you-eat-more-or-not-at-all/.

9. Stress in America 2021, "One Year Later, a New Wave of Pandemic Health Concerns."

10. Health Essentials, "Why You Shouldn't Rely on Alcohol During Times of Stress," Cleveland Clinic, April 16, 2020, https://health.clevelandclinic.org/alcohol-during-times-of-stress/.

11. Patrick Van Kessel et al., "In Their Own Words, Americans Describe the Struggles and Silver Linings of the COVID-19 Pandemic," Pew Research Center, March 5, 2021, https://www.pewresearch.org/2021/03/05/in-their-own-words-americans-describe-the-struggles-and-silver-linings-of-the-covid-19-pandemic/.

12. William A. Haseltine, "One Fifth of Adults Report a Relationship Breakdown During the Pandemic," *Forbes*, August 31, 2021, https://www.forbes.com/sites/williamhaseltine/2021/08/31/one-fifth-of-adults-report-a-relationship-breakdown-during-the-pandemic/.

13. Daniel A. Cox, "The State of American Friendship: Change, Challenges, and Loss," Survey Center on American Life, June 8, 2021, https://www.americansurveycenter.org/research/the-state-of-american-friendship-change-challenges-and-loss/.

14. McDougall, "Secrets of the Tarahumara."

Chapter 4

1. Steven Furtick, "Green Light at the Red Sea, Pastor Steven Furtick, Elevation Church," Elevation Church, streamed live September 12, 2021, YouTube video, 58:41, https://www.youtube.com/watch?v=ktVg3HCSsrY.

2. Simon Sinek, "Simon Sinek: Understanding the Game We're Playing," CreativeMornings HQ, October 16, 2016, YouTube video, 30:20, https://www.youtube.com/watch?v=sjxNTcsquG8.

3. Simon Sinek, "Simon Sinek: Understanding the Game."

4. Tucker C. Toole, "Here's the History of Basketball—from Peach Baskets in Springfield to Global Phenomenon," *National Geographic*, March 27, 2021, https://www.nationalgeographic

.com/history/article/basketball-only-major-sport-invented
-united-states-how-it-was-created.

5. Grant Freeland, "Talent Wins Games, Teamwork Wins
Championships," *Forbes*, June 1, 2018, https://www.forbes.com
/sites/grantfreeland/2018/06/01/talent-wins-games-teamwork
-wins-championships/.

6. Phil Moore, *Straight to the Heart of Moses: 60 Bite–Sized Insights
from Exodus, Leviticus, Numbers, and Deuteronomy* (Grand
Rapids, MI: Monarch, 2011), 33.

Chapter 5

1. "Fascinating and Amazing Human Body Facts and Trivia,"
Disabled World, June 11, 2015, https://www.disabled-world
.com/medical/human-body-facts.php.

2. Ari Hahn, "That Will Teach You! Why Punishment Damages
Relationships," Choose Help, updated June 1, 2014, https://
www.choosehelp.com/topics/couples-counseling
/that-will-teach-you-why-punishment-damages-relationships.

3. Hahn, "That Will Teach You!"

4. Peg Streep, "Why Words Can Hurt at Least as Much as Sticks
and Stones," *Psychology Today*, August 20, 2013, https://www
.psychologytoday.com/us/blog/tech-support/201308/why-words
-can-hurt-least-much-sticks-and-stones.

5. Streep, "Why Words Can Hurt."

6. C. Nathan Dewall et al., "Acetaminophen Reduces Social Pain:
Behavioral and Neural Evidence," *Psychological Science* 21, no. 7
(July 2010): 931–37, https://doi.org/10.1177/0956797610374741.

7. T. D. Jakes, "Get Your Own Oil! - Bishop T.D. Jakes," T.D.
Jakes, July 18, 2021, YouTube video, 1:19:23, https://www
.youtube.com/watch?v=HlbgI1rScJc&t=2968s.

8. John McKinley, "Metaphors Revealing the Holy Spirit, Part 3:
Oil as a Metaphor for the Holy Spirit," The Good Book Blog,
March 28, 2016, https://www.biola.edu/blogs/good-book
-blog/2016/metaphors-revealing-the-holy-spirit-part-3-oil-as-a
-metaphor-for-the-holy-spirit.

9. Jakes, "Get Your Own Oil!"

10. Jim Camp, *Start with No: The Negotiating Tools That the Pros Want You to Know* (New York: Crown Business, 2002).

Chapter 6

1. See Charles Dickens, *The Strange Gentleman: "A Very Little Key Will Open a Very Heavy Door"* (1836; repr., n.p.: Stage Door, 2013).

2. Bessel A. van der Kolk, *The Body Keeps the Score: Brain, Mind and Body in the Healing of Trauma* (New York: Viking, 2014), 29–30.

3. Kolk, *Body Keeps the Score*, 30.

4. Kolk, *Body Keeps the Score*, 30–31.

5. Irina Bancos, "What Is Serotonin?," Hormone Health Network, December 2018.

6. Don Norman, *The Design of Everyday Things*, rev. ed. (New York: Basic Books, 2013).

7. Joseph A. DeVito, *The Interpersonal Communication Book*, 16th ed. (Hoboken, NJ: Pearson, 2021).

8. Jen Wolkin (@drjenwolkin), "Trauma changes the brain AND SO. DOES. HEALING.," Twitter, January 22, 2022, 6:25 p.m., https://twitter.com/drjenwolkin/status/1485061038689198085?s=21.

Chapter 7

1. Kristen Nunez, "Fight, Flight, Freeze: What This Response Means," Healthline, February 21, 2020, https://www.healthline.com/health/mental-health/fight-flight-freeze.

2. Nunez, "Fight, Flight, Freeze."

3. Rachael Sharman, "Why Do We Freeze When We're Scared?," *Popular Science*, October 12, 2017, https://www.popsci.com/why-do-we-freeze-when-frightened/.

4. Heather Thompson Day (@HeatherTDay), "Seeing a theme so I'd like to take an informal poll: What has covid hurt more?"

Twitter, September 13, 2021, 10:26 a.m., https://twitter.com /HeatherTDay/status/1437422328711991304?s=20.

5. Kendra Cherry, "5 Surprising Ways That Stress Affects Your Brain," Verywell Mind, April 8, 2021, https://www .verywellmind.com/surprising-ways-that-stress-affects-your -brain-2795040.

6. Karen Young, "The Effects of Toxic Stress on the Brain & Body—How to Heal & Protect," Hey Sigmund, accessed February 19, 2022, https://www.heysigmund.com/toxic-stress/.

7. Andrew Newberg and Mark Robert Waldman, *Words Can Change Your Brain: 12 Conversation Strategies to Build Trust, Resolve Conflict, and Increase Intimacy* (New York: Hudson Street Press, 2012), 24–25.

8. Alison Escalante, "Here's How Science Says You Can Give the Perfect Hug (Once Social Distancing Is Over)," *Forbes*, June 9, 2020, https://www.forbes.com/sites/alisonescalante/2020/06/09 /how-to-give-the-perfect-hug-according-to-science/.

9. Kerstin Uvnas-Moberg and Maria Petersson, "Oxytocin, a Mediator of Anti-stress, Well-being, Social Interaction, Growth and Healing," *Zeitschrift fur Psychosomatische Medizin und Psychotherapie* 51, no. 1 (2005): 57–80, https://pubmed.ncbi.nlm .nih.gov/15834840/.

10. Erica Cirino, "What Are the Benefits of Hugging?," Healthline, April 11, 2018, https://www.healthline.com/health /hugging-benefits#2.-Hugs-may-protect-you-against-illness.

11. Emily Ho, "Embrace the 20 Second Hug for Better Health," Enell, May 24, 2019, https://enell.com/blogs/blog /embrace-the-20-second-hug-for-better-health.

12. Stephanie Pappas and Ailsa Harvey, "Oxytocin: Facts About the 'Cuddle Hormone,'" LiveScience, October 27, 2021, https:// www.livescience.com/42198-what-is-oxytocin.html.

13. Charles M. Sell, *Family Ministry* (Grand Rapids, MI: Zondervan, 1995).

14. Sell, *Family Ministry*, 134.

15. Earl E. Bakken Center for Spirituality and Healing, "Why Personal Relationships Are Important," University of Minnesota, accessed February 19, 2022, https://www .takingcharge.csh.umn .edu/why-personal-relationships-are-important.

16. Earl E. Bakken Center for Spirituality and Healing, "Why Personal Relationships Are Important."

17. Claire Pomeroy, "Loneliness Is Harmful to Our Nation's Health," *Scientific American*, March 20, 2019, https://blogs .scientificamerican.com/observations/loneliness-is-harmful -to-our-nations-health/.

18. Alexander Nehamas and Paul Woodruff, *Symposium: Plato* (Indianapolis: Hackett, 1989).

19. Agustín Fuentes, "What Is Love?," *Psychology Today*, August 14, 2012, https://www.psychologytoday.com/us/blog/busting-myths -about-human-nature/201208/what-is-love.

20. Fuentes, "What Is Love?"

21. Fuentes, "What Is Love?"

Chapter 8

1. F. F. Bruce, *Romans: An Introduction and Commentary* (Downers Grove, IL: IVP Academic, 2007), 167.

2. Seth Michael Day (@SethMDay), "I got kicked out for smoking pot in the gym bathroom of my private Christian high school," Twitter, March 23, 2020, 11:05 a.m., https://twitter.com /sethmday/status/1242105118318907392.

3. Steve Cuss, "Heather Thompson Day," October 18, 2021, in *Managing Leadership Anxiety: Yours and Theirs*, podcast, MP3 audio, 50:00, https://podcasts.apple.com/pa/podcast/s7e9 -heather-thompson-day/id1441812273?i=1000538924469&l=en.

4. National Center for Injury Prevention and Control, Division of Violence Prevention, "Adverse Childhood Experiences (ACEs)," Centers for Disease Control and Prevention, April 2, 2021, https://www.cdc.gov/violenceprevention/aces/index.html.

5. Michael G. Quirke, "What Are the 10 ACEs of Trauma & How Can You Begin to Face Them?," MichaelGQuirke.com, March 22, 2021, https://michaelgquirke.com/what-are-the-10 -aces-of-trauma-how-can-you-begin-to-face-them/.

6. "Got Your ACE Score?" ACE's Connection Network, accessed March 17, 2022, PDF, https://www.scls.info/files/ce/program /Blog/GotYourACE.pdf.

7. "Take the ACES Quiz," American Society for the Positive Care of Children, September 30, 2021, https://americanspcc.org /take-the-aces-quiz/.

8. "The Consequences of Childhood Trauma," Byron Clinic and Trauma Resolution, accessed February 19, 2022, https:// byronclinic.com/finding-your-ace-score/.

9. Van der Kolk, *Body Keeps the Score: Brain, Mind and Body in the Healing of Trauma* (New York: Viking, 2014).

10. Brené Brown, *Braving the Wilderness: The Quest for True Belonging and the Courage to Stand Alone* (New York: Random House, 2017).

11. Shannon Thomas, *Healing from Hidden Abuse: A Journey Through the Stages of Recovery from Psychological Abuse* (Scottsdale, AZ: MAST Publishing House, 2016).

12. David Richo, *Daring to Trust: Opening Ourselves to Real Love and Intimacy* (Boston: Shambhala, 2010).

13. James H. Cone, *The Cross and the Lynching Tree* (Maryknoll, NY: Orbis Books, 2011).

14. Nadine Burke Harris, "How Childhood Trauma Affects Health Across a Lifetime: Nadine Burke Harris," TED, February 17, 2015, YouTube video, 16:02, https://youtu.be/95ovIJ3dsNk.

15. Brené Brown, "The Power of Vulnerability: Brené Brown," TED, January 3, 2011, YouTube video, 20:49, https://www .youtube.com/watch?v=iCvmsMzlF7o.

Chapter 9

1. Tim Wigmore, "Why Are Great Athletes More Likely to Be Younger Siblings?," FiveThirtyEight, December 1, 2020, https://fivethirtyeight.com/features/why-are-great-athletes-more-likely -to-be-the-younger-siblings/; see also A. Mark Williams and Tim Wigmore, *The Best: How Elite Athletes Are Made* (Boston: Nicholas Brealey Publishing, 2020).

2. Wigmore, "Why Are Great Athletes More Likely to Be Younger Siblings?"

3. "Episode 2 of the Last Dance, Showed How Michael Jordan Became Michael Jordan," NBC Sports, accessed March 17, 2022, https://www.nbcsports.com/chicago/bulls/episode-2-last -dance-showed-how-michael-jordan-became-michael-jordan.

4. "The Last Dance: Michael Jordan Stories That Didn't Make Final Cut," NBC Sports, May 18, 2020, https://www.nbcsports .com/chicago/bulls/last-dance-michael-jordan-stories-didnt -make-final-cut.

5. Claire Pomeroy, "Loneliness Is Harmful to Our Nation's Health," *Scientific American*, March 20, 2019, https://blogs .scientificamerican.com/observations/loneliness-is-harmful -to-our-nations-health/.

6. Nicole Spector, "How to Train Your Brain to Accept Change, According to Neuroscience," NBC News, November 12, 2018, https://www.nbcnews.com/better/health/how-train-your-brain -accept-change-according-neuroscience-ncna934011.

7. Quoted in Spector, "How to Train Your Brain."

8. Leading Effectively Staff, "How to Transition Through Change," Center for Creative Leadership, November 16, 2020, https://www.ccl.org/articles/leading-effectively-articles /adapting-to-change-its-about-the-transition/.

9. Alan Deutschman, "Change or Die," *Fast Company*, May 1, 2005, https://www.fastcompany.com/52717/change-or-die.

10. Mark S. Granovetter, "The Strength of Weak Ties," *American*

Journal of Sociology 78, no. 6 (May 1973): 1360–80, https://doi
.org/10.1086/225469.

11. Heather Thompson Day (@HeatherTDay), "I teach social
    media," Twitter, July 30, 2020, 8:12 p.m., https://twitter.com
    /HeatherTDay/status/1288990804552318979?s=20.

12. Ian Leslie, "Why Your 'Weak-Tie' Friendships May Mean More
    Than You Think," BBC, July 2, 2020, https://www.bbc.com
    /worklife/article/20200701-why-your-weak-tie-friendships-may
    -mean-more-than-you-think.

13. Chrissy Teigen (@chrissyteigen), "I talk to everyone and I like
    everyone?" Twitter, July 30, 2020, 8:36 p.m., https://twitter.com
    /chrissyteigen/status/1288996874439933952?s=20.

14. Claire Pomeroy, "Loneliness Is Harmful to Our Nation's
    Health," Scientific American, March 20, 2019, https://blogs
    .scientificamerican.com/observations/loneliness-is-harmful-to
    -our-nations-health/.

15. "'It's Destiny!' Most Americans Believe in Soul Mates," Marist
    Poll, February 10, 2011, http://maristpoll.marist.edu/210
    -its-destiny-most-americans-believe-in-soul-mates/#sthash
    .dYxrOKMW.dpbs.

16. C. Raymond Knee and Kristen N. Petty, "Implicit Theories
    of Relationships: Destiny and Growth Beliefs," in *The Oxford
    Handbook of Close Relationships*, ed. Jeffrey A. Simpson and
    Lorne Campbell (New York: Oxford University Press, 2013).

17. Dale Carnegie, *How to Win Friends and Influence People* (1936;
    repr., London: Arcturus, 2021), 88.

18. Alison Wood Brooks and Leslie K. John, "The Surprising
    Power of Questions," *Harvard Business Review*, May–June 2018,
    https://hbr.org/2018/05/the-surprising-power-of-questions.

Chapter 10

1. Lysa TerKeurst, *Forgiving What You Can't Forget: Discover How
   to Move On, Make Peace with Painful Memories, and Create a Life
   That's Beautiful Again* (Nashville: Thomas Nelson, 2020). See

also Luke 7:47. Those who experience forgiveness can give it. What if we do the process backward? We try to will ourselves to forgive the other, but we can't because we haven't forgiven ourselves. Forgiveness creates more forgiveness.

2. "Forgiveness: Your Health Depends on It," Johns Hopkins Medicine, accessed February 19, 2022, https://www .hopkinsmedicine.org/health/wellness-and-prevention /forgiveness-your-health-depends-on-it.

3. "Forgiveness: Your Health Depends on It," Johns Hopkins Medicine.

4. StrategyOne, "Survey of Love and Forgiveness in American Society," Fetzer Institute, October 2010, https://fetzer.org /sites/default/files/images/resources/attachment/%5Bcurrent -date%3Atiny%5D/Survey%20of%20Love%20and%20 Forgiveness%20in%20American%20Society%20Report.pdf.

5. Research Release in Faith & Christianity, "1 in 4 Practicing Christians Struggles to Forgive Someone," Barna Group, April 11, 2019, https://www.barna.com/research /forgiveness-christians/.

6. Justin Giboney, Michael Wear, and Chris Butler, *Compassion (&) Conviction: The AND Campaign's Guide to Faithful Civic Engagement* (Downers Grove, IL: InterVarsity Press, 2020).

Chapter 11

1. Brooke Kato, "What Is Cancel Culture? Everything to Know about the Toxic Online Trend," *New York Post*, August 31, 2021, https://nypost.com/article/what-is-cancel-culture-breaking -down-the-toxic-online-trend.

2. Jon Ronson, "How One Stupid Tweet Ruined Justine Sacco's Life," *New York Times Magazine*, February 15, 2015, https:// www.nytimes.com/2015/02/15/magazine/how-one-stupid -tweet-ruined-justine-saccos-life.html.

3. Martin Luther King Jr., "Chapter 27: Watts," The Martin Luther King, Jr. Research and Education Institute, accessed

February 19, 2022, https://kinginstitute.stanford.edu/king
-papers/publications/autobiography-martin-luther-king-jr
-contents/chapter-27-watts.

4. Excerpt from Martin Luther King Jr., *Where Do We Go from Here: Chaos or Community?* (New York: Harper & Row, 1967), cited by The King Legacy, http://www.thekinglegacy.org/books /where-do-we-go-here-chaos-or-community.

5. King, *Where Do We Go from Here?*.

6. Martin Luther King Jr., "Our God Is Marching On!," The Martin Luther King Jr. Research and Education Institute, March 25, 1965, https://kinginstitute.stanford.edu/our -god-marching.

7. Stephan A. Schwartz, "Police Brutality and Racism in America," *Explore* 16, no. 5 (September–October 2020): 280–82, https:// doi.org/10.1016/j.explore.2020.06.010.

8. James C. Cobb, "Even Though He Is Revered Today, MLK Was Widely Disliked by the American Public When He Was Killed," *Smithsonian Magazine*, April 4, 2018, https://www .smithsonianmag.com/history/why-martin-luther-king-had-75 -percent-disapproval-rating-year-he-died-180968664/.

9. Milenko Martinovich, "Americans' Partisan Identities Are Stronger than Race and Ethnicity, Stanford Scholar Finds," Stanford News, August 31, 2017, https://news.stanford .edu/2017/08/31/political-party-identities-stronger-race-religion/.

10. Geoffrey L. Cohen, "Party Over Policy: The Dominating Impact of Group Influence on Political Beliefs," *Journal of Personality and Social Psychology* 85, no. 5 (November 2003): 808–22, https://doi.org/10.1037/0022-3514.85.5.808.

11. Jonah Berger, *Invisible Influence: The Hidden Forces That Shape Behavior* (New York: Simon & Schuster, 2016).

12. "Mahatma Gandhi Says He Believes in Christ but Not Christianity," *Harvard Crimson*, January 11, 1927, https://www .thecrimson.com/article/1927/1/11/mahatma-gandhi-says-he -believes-in/.

13. Martin Luther King Jr., "Beyond Vietnam: A Time to Break Silence," April 4, 1967, American Rhetoric: Online Speech Bank, https://www.americanrhetoric.com/speeches /mlkatimetobreaksilence.htm.
14. King, "Beyond Vietnam."
15. King, "Beyond Vietnam."
16. King, "Beyond Vietnam: A Time to Break Silence," MLK, Riverside Church Speech, accessed December 21, 2021, http:// inside.sfuhs.org/dept/history/US_History_reader/Chapter14 /MLKriverside.htm.

Chapter 12

1. Kathryn Dill, "In '*Option B*,' Sheryl Sandberg Presents Meaningful Work as an Antidote to Trauma," CNBC, May 3, 2017, https://www.cnbc.com/2017/05/03/in-option-b-sheryl -sandberg-presents-work-as-an-antidote-to-trauma.html.
2. Sheryl Sandberg and Adam Grant, *Option B: Facing Adversity, Building Resilience, and Finding Joy* (New York: Alfred A. Knopf, 2017), 87.
3. Dill, "*Option B*."
4. Sandberg and Grant, *Option B*, 92.

Conclusion

1. "Relationships Make College Experience, Poll Finds," *The Times-News*, August 25, 2018, https://www .thetimesnews.com/news/20180825/elon-poll-relationships -make-college-experience.
2. Paula Burkes, "Most Workplace Friendships Stay at the Office, New Study Says," *Oklahoma City Oklahoman*, September 12, 2018, https://www.oklahoman.com/story/business /columns/2018/09/12/americans-average-define-percent -their-workers-workers-percent-consider-least-their-workers -bestie/60502189007/.
3. Alison Doyle, "What Is the Average Hours Per Week Worked

in the US?," The Balance Careers, January 25, 2021, https://
www.thebalancecareers.com/what-is-the-average-hours-per
-week-worked-in-the-us-2060631.

4. Eric Zorn, "Without Failure, Jordan Would Be False Idol,"
   Chicago Tribune, May 19, 1997, https://www.chicagotribune
   .com/news/ct-xpm-1997-05-19-9705190096-story.html.

Acknowledgments

To our children, London, Hudson, and Sawyer, may you never forget the Day family rule: we stick together.

To our families, thank you for showing us what relationships that don't quit look like. You have truly been the backbone of our lives. We are in debt to you for your prayers, tears, and support of this book. We are who we are because of you.

To our friends, thank you for every phone call, text, walk, late-night laugh, and early morning coffee. To have friends that become family has been the Lord's greatest gift to us.

To Jose Rojas, thank you for sitting on the phone with us past midnight. For prayers that felt like balm, and advice that changed our course. Your mentorship has changed our development.

To our agent, Amanda Luedeke, you signed us both many, many years ago. With no platform, no sales numbers, and no prospects. You believed in us. You are more than an agent. You are a dear friend.

To our editors, Kyle Olund, Jennifer McNeil, and Lauren Bridges, we could not have asked for a better team. You took a concept and helped us turn it into a book we are incredibly proud of. Thank you for pushing us, challenging us, and encouraging us.

To our publisher, W Publishing, and Damon Reiss, thank you for taking a chance on us—for seeing a future for us we couldn't see for ourselves.

To Lysa TerKeurst and the COMPEL training team, we constantly came back to your time, wisdom, and direction in this writing process. It was invaluable.

To all our sources in this book, without your research and insights this book wouldn't exist. Thank you for bringing so much to the conversation.

About the Authors

Heather Thompson Day is an Associate Professor of Communication at Andrews University. She is passionate about supporting women and runs an online community called *I'm That Wife*, which has over two hundred thousand followers. Heather's writing has been featured on outlets like *TODAY* and the National Communication Association. She has been interviewed by BBC Radio Live and has been featured in *Forbes*. She believes her calling is to stand in the gaps of our churches for young people. She is the author of seven books, including *It's Not Your Turn* and *Confessions of a Christian Wife*.

Seth Day is a graduate student of educational psychology. He has been a pastor and campus chaplain. His background in human service counseling and ministry brings an important spiritual component to this book. Seth and Heather reside in St. Joseph, Michigan, with their three children, London, Hudson, and Sawyer.